REVELATION AND INSPIRATION

REVELATION AND INSPIRATION

BY

JAMES ORR

BAKER BOOK HOUSE
Grand Rapids, Michigan

Reprinted 1969 by
Baker Book House Company

Library of Congress Catalog Card Number: 74-100535

Reprinted from the
original printing made
in 1910 by Duckworth
and Company, London

PHOTOLITHOPRINTED BY CUSHING - MALLOY, INC.
ANN ARBOR, MICHIGAN, UNITED STATES OF AMERICA
1969

INTRODUCTION

by Addison H. Leitch

Most agree that it was T. S. Eliot's introduction to Dante's *The Divine Comedy* which set in motion the revival of Dante studies in this century. One could hope that this sort of thing could happen for many of the theological writers of former days, and especially for the writings of James Orr. Discussing theology with a man whose judgment I very highly respect, the names of P. T. Forsyth and James Orr were before us. It was my contention that the mass of writing produced by P. T. Forsyth was probably the greatest theological library produced in our generation, while my friend insisted that the contributions of James Orr were greater. His argument was that James Orr's work was certainly as profound and surely as interesting as that of P. T. Forsyth, but that Orr had shown himself to be master over a wider variety of topics. Without minimizing at all my enthusiasm for Forsyth, I must admit that what my friend said about Orr without question marks the man. He has indeed proved himself to be the absolute master on a whole series of theological issues.

Revelation and Inspiration is representative of this mastery.

The writing of James Orr came when Great Britain was being flooded with higher critical German scholarship. It was not until a later date that German scholarship found direct access to American theology, and it is generally agreed that American theology discovered German scholarship by way of Scotch and English writers. What was most disturbing in this process was that many who were enamored of German scholarship and many others who wished to be known as leaders in the new learning, accepted all too easily anything which arrived with the German imprimatur. Very few conservative scholars had either the scholarship, the breadth of understanding, and the mastery of the languages to defend a conservative position which other scholars could accept. James Orr was one who had the gifts, who was capable of facing the arguments of the critics, and who indeed did. A significant sentence which appears in *Revelation and Inspiration* illustrates his attitude: "This verdict may very reasonably be challenged." While so many others seemed to accept the unexamined truth of "the findings of assured scholarship," James Orr insisted on taking another look. He was not panicked by degrees, titles, university names or a German accent. And when he had reasonably challenged the findings of the higher critics, he in turn urged them, indeed begged them, to criticize his own approach. This they never did, as was true of Machen's works at a later date. Orr's writings were bypassed and are still waiting to be answered by those who have dominated the theological field for the last sixty years.

The Problem of the Old Testament is a case in point. "Everyone knows" that the approach to the Old Testament in criticism and understanding is by the acceptance in general of the E,J,P,D sources. If the acceptance of this approach necessitates the rearrangement of the Old Testament books, or requires that what appears early actually came late, or that we cannot have monotheism before Moses, even though Abraham appears in Genesis, so much the worse for the Old Testament. With meticulous scholarship Orr opposed this view and made his own case. Since the book was never answered, how can anyone claim mastery in this field today if he bypasses Orr. So with the book *The Virgin Birth*. Generations of seminarians now have come from our schools with the quiet assumption that nothing can be said for believing in such a phenomenon. They have been taught not to believe in it, and this coupled with the difficulty of the belief itself, plus the fact that those who do believe it must surely be a little gullible, makes it easy for them to dismiss it out of hand. I am not arguing here that a seminary graduate may not deny the virgin birth. I am arguing, however, that he has no right to deny it if he has not read James Or.

Revelation and Inspiration has this same authority in spite of its appearance sixty years ago. It still faces the modern reader with the inescapable fact of its existence. One simply cannot, in my judgment, approach either revelation or inspiration without meeting the arguments which Orr has here set forth. Here again his treatment is marked by a meticulous concern for every phase of the problem. One is greatly helped by the clarity of the distinctions which he makes. He makes it perfectly clear what is meant and what is not meant by the various positions offered, and then makes very clear his presentation of the orthodox position. He never attempts to set up straw men nor does he make a caricature of his opponent's position in order to destroy it by scorn. This is all too easy. He is complete master of the sources for the wide variety of position which he opposes and for the position which he supports; and although he is very free in his use of sources (this is one mark of his mastery), he insists in his arguments on using the most revered and established of those who hold contrary positions. He is devastating, however, in his use of the *argumentum ad hominem.* Thus by using the most authoritative opponents and turning their argument back upon them he does indeed challenge assumptions as well as arguments. All this he does, however, in a gentle and responsible fashion. His books are free from polemics and the bitterness which this often creates.

The sweetness of spirit evidenced in this book makes of it, in certain classic portions, a useful book for devotions. Time and again Orr's arguments lead him into discussions of other topics which in turn leads him to an overall view of some phase of our faith where his own spiritual magnificance comes through. The book is also an excellent source book for helpful approaches to a wide variety of topics beyond the subject itself; e.g., miracles, angels, natural disasters, the Kenosis, the person of Christ, cruelty in warfare and the like. His use of Scripture for argument and illustration is a source of constant delight.

The question naturally arises in the re-publication of a book sixty years old, what possible value it can have in the theological ferment of our own day. The same, of course, could be said of the revival of almost any classic in almost any field. Some problems are perennial. Once answers are given to these problems, if they are sound it the first place, they remain sound in spite of shifts in emphasis and the amazing increase in knowledge in the various disciplines. Some questions and some answers abide; this, therefore, is the merit of *Revelation and Inspiration.* A careful reading of it for the first time will surprise most readers by virtue of its modernity and relevance.

Revelation, as the title suggests, is treated first. It is in this general area that Orr is speaking to the liberals of our day, however loosely that word may be construed, because most liberal theologians in this century have been concerned with revelation rather than with inspiration. It is impossible, of course, for Orr to be writing about Barth, Brunner, Niebuhr, Tillich, Bonhoeffer or even John A. T. Robinson. What is surprising, however, is that what appears to be modern theology today is over and over again a re-working of the same problems which were Orr's problems at the turn of the century. Increasingly it is being recognized that liberal theology in our day takes its lead from Kant's epistemology and Schleiermacher's theology. At least it has appeared to me that an understanding of Kant and Schleiermacher makes most modern theology more understandable in approach, in problems and in sources. Thus the arguments of *Revelation and Inspiration* with Orr's understanding of 19th Century theology and philosophy make him quite relevant to the theological breakthrough which began with Barth. In fact, written when it was, it throws a special light on studies now.

Whereas Orr's work on revelation will enlighten the liberal, his work on inspiration should enlighten the conservative. There is no question that the doctrine of Scripture lies at the center of all arguments among the conservatives and none more apparently than what view should be taken of verbal inerrancy. James Orr does not support verbal inerrancy, but as P. T. Forsyth once said of himself, he is so close to it that it is hard to see the distinction. He argues that verbal inerrancy is untenable and shows us why. Meanwhile he takes nothing away from the absolute authority of Holy Writ. There is no shading into Barth's Word. Supporting the words as well as the Word there is staunch, although careful, support of the authority of the Bible throughout. As one has no right to oppose the virgin birth without having read Orr, so no one has the right to dismiss the objective reality of the words themselves nor on the other hand insist on verbal inerrancy until he has read James Orr.

If one supposes that Orr's *Revelation and Inspiration* is not for him, then in the words of Orr again, "This verdict may very reasonably be challenged".

PREFACE

This volume is written under the conviction that revelation and inspiration, in connection with the Bible, can only be defended in conjunction with a more positive view of the structure of the Bible itself than is at present prevalent. The three things imply each other—a positive view of the structure of the Bible, the recognition of a true supernatural revelation in its history, and a belief, in accordance with the teaching of Christ and His apostles, in the inspiration of the record. The evidence for each of these three things yields support to faith in the other two. The critical appreciation of the Bible is helped by the recognition of the revelation contained in it, and of the character of inspiration attaching to the book which is the vehicle of the revelation. The revelation sustains faith in inspiration, and *vice versâ*. From the unity of the three aspects results the conception of a *Holy Scripture.*

CONTENTS

CHAPTER I

CHAPTER II

CHAPTER III

CHAPTER IV

CHAPTER V

CHAPTER VI

CHAPTER VII

CHAPTER VIII

CHAPTER IX

CHAPTER X

REVELATION AND INSPIRATION

CHAPTER I

REVELATION AND INSPIRATION IN CURRENT THOUGHT—MODERN STANDPOINTS

THERE is perhaps no subject at the present moment more difficult to write upon, and above all to write upon wisely, than this of Revelation and Inspiration. Have we an authoritative divine revelation in the Bible ? Is the Bible itself, in a unique and special sense, an inspired book ? What are the limits of this inspiration, and how does it differ from the inspiration we ascribe to poets and other men of genius ? Or is there a difference of kind at all ? The many able books which have recently been written on this subject probably help more to reveal the difficulties connected with it than to furnish a practical and satisfactory solution of these difficulties. Where others have come short, it is not easy to hope that the present writer will succeed.

It may be a useful opening of the inquiry to investigate at the outset some of the various senses in which the terms Revelation and Inspiration, with which we are to be occupied, are employed, and the relations in which the ideas they represent stand to the general thought of the age.

I. Revelation and Religion.

It is customary to speak of the decay of faith in divine revelation, and in the sense intended, such a weakening of faith must be acknowledged. In a wider respect, there is probably no proposition on which the higher religious philosophy of the past hundred years is more agreed than this—that all *religion originates in revelation.* Man can know God only as, in some way, God reveals, or makes Himself known, to man.[1] The questions on which division arises are—What is the nature or manner of this revelation ? How is it brought about ? Is it natural simply, or is it also supernatural ? And what do these terms—' natural ' and ' supernatural ' —in this connection themselves import ?

1. It is indeed singular to observe the fascination which this idea of *revelation* (*Offenbarung*) has for thinkers of all schools in the later philosophy of religion. This is specially the case in Germany—the country from which most of the newer impulses which have entered theology have proceeded. In Fichte, and Schelling, and Hegel ; in Schleiermacher and Rothe ; in speculative theologians like Biedermann and Pfleiderer ; in Old Testament critical scholars like Schultz and Smend ; in theologians of positive type like Dorner ; in the newer theology of Ritschl, the idea of God as self-revealing, and of religion, including of course Christianity, as resting on revelation, may be said to be fundamental. Even where, as in Hegel, or in the earlier phases of Schleiermacher's thinking, God

[1] Cf. *e.g.* Pfleiderer, *Phil. of Rel.* iii. pp. 46 ff. (E.T.) ; Dorner, *System of Doct.* ii. pp. 133 ff. (E.T.).

is more or less pantheistically conceived, a foremost place is given to this idea. In Hegel, it is of the essence of spirit to reveal itself, and Christianity, as the religion in which God and the consciousness of Himself become one in man—in which Spirit rises to the consciousness of identity with itself—is the Absolute or 'Revealed' religion.[1]

2. As springing from this tendency to recognise revelation as everywhere the basis of religion, is next to be noted, in connection with the prominence now given to the comparative study of religion, the rise of a disposition to extend the idea of revelation *to all the forms of historical religion*, and to regard these as simply more or less perfect stages in an ascent of which the religion of Israel, and the development of this into Christianity, form, thus far, the summit. This, as will be seen after, is a special feature in the new 'religious-historical' way of contemplating the spiritual development of mankind. Distinction, naturally, is made between higher and lower, cruder and more intelligent, grosser and more spiritual, types of religion; but no absolute line, it is held, can be drawn by the historical investigator between 'revealed' and 'non-revealed' religions. All must be viewed as

[1] Cf. Hegel, *Religionsphilosophie*, ii. pp. 191 ff. Schelling has his two volumes of the *Philosophie der Offenbarung*.

A curious illustration of the persistence and influence of this idea is afforded by the pessimist Von Hartmann, the philosopher of 'The Unconscious,' who takes over into his Philosophy of Religion the whole nomenclature of Christianity, descanting among other things on 'Grace and Faith,' 'The Grace of Revelation and Intellectual Faith' (*Die Religion des Geistes*, pp. 64, 74 ff.). Among the sub-headings are 'External and Inner Revelation,' 'Traditional and Personal Revelation,' 'The Originality of Revelation,' 'The Truth of Revelation,' etc.

stages in the general upward movement of the human spirit under the impulse of the divine Spirit. To this advance every factor in the culture of humanity contributes.[1] It is at the same time significant that even among those whose general sympathies are with this standpoint, a tendency is manifest to claim for the religions of Israel and Christ, in a peculiar sense, the designation of religions of 'revelation.' Gunkel, a sufficiently radical Old Testament critic, yet writes, 'Israel is, and remains, the people of revelation.'[2] Herrmann, of the Ritschlian school, emphasises the fact of historical revelation in Christ almost to the exclusion of revelation anywhere else.[3]

3. With respect to this universalising of the idea of revelation, on which more will be said hereafter, the general principle on which it rests may be granted, with one important qualification, viz., that all *true* religion originates in revelation. For it is not here to be overlooked that 'religion' is a wide word, and covers much which is self-evidently false, foolish, and superstitious—in no way the product of revelation, either general or special, but the outcome only of man's wayward and unbridled phantasy. If the savage worships fetishes, or ghosts, or totems, — if, through an animistic impulse, he peoples heaven and earth with number-

[1] W. Bousset, in his book translated under the title *What is Religion?* observes: 'The distinction between natural and revealed religion is impossible. . . . Christianity is not the one religion, the only religion, but simply the most complete species of the genus' (pp. 8, 9). See also the remarks of the translator in the preface to the work.

[2] *Israel und Babylonien*, pp. 37-8.

[3] Cf. his *Communion with God*, passim.

less imaginary spirits,—if he frames the image of a tribal god, and carves a stick or stone into some hideous shape to embody his conception of his deity,—one is compelled to withhold assent from the proposition that all this rests on revelation. It becomes necessary to make an important distinction. Let it be granted, what is involved in a true philosophy of religion, that there is in man that which impels him in search of an infinite; granted, what is likewise true, that there is that in nature, and in man's own soul, which awakens in him the *sense* or *feeling* of the infinite (*sensus numinis*), it cannot be justly disputed that the ideas of God which spring from this source contain in them an element of revelation.[1] Even where the religion rises no higher than nature-worship—the worship of sun, sky, fire, or other natural phenomena—there is this element of revelation—this sense of a deity felt to pervade all, at the basis. Lower down, so far as any trace of this original intuition cleaves to the savage's conception of his fetish, idol, or spirit, that glimmer of truth in his religion comes from revelation. Generally, however, it is precisely this higher element which the ordinary psychological theories of religion tend to ignore. Man's religious ideas are sought to be accounted for by purely subjective causes—animism, belief in ghosts, and the like—and the spirits with which the world is filled have no more reality than the gnomes and fairies of our nursery story-books. They stand in a quite distinct category from ideas which have their source in 'revelation,' even in the widest sense of that word, and ought not to be confounded with them.

[1] Cf. Rom. i 20.

II. Natural and Supernatural in Revelation.

More fundamental, as marking a dividing-line between parties on this subject, is the question whether, as the 'modern' school avers, religion is only of the natural character now indicated, or whether a distinction is not to be made between this, and religion proceeding from a higher and more special source—a *super*natural as distinguished from a simply *natural* revelation. This is the vital question into which, at the present time, all other questions with regard to revelation and inspiration will be found to resolve themselves. It is, at the same time, a question wrapped up in so many ambiguities, and implicated with so many subtleties, that it is by no means easy to rid the discussion of it of irrelevances, and present it to the mind as a clear and simple issue.

1. An ambiguity, which it is important to observe, lurks on the threshold in the word 'supernatural' itself. It is not unusual, and in the sense in which the terms are used is not incorrect, to express *the point at issue* between opposing schools by saying that it is a question of *the admission or the denial of the supernatural.* The very last thing, however, which writers of the modern school would admit is, that they are fairly charged with denying the supernatural. In the fullest sense, they will tell you, they acknowledge, nay contend for, the supernatural. It is the distinction itself between 'natural' and 'supernatural' which, in the interests of what they take to be a higher point of view, they seek to break down. There is, they affirm, a supernatural basis of the universe, and a supernatural

presence and action of God in its every part. Only, they will say, it is a supernatural which is not distinct from nature, but which expresses itself *in* nature's own forces and laws, and in the orderly course of nature's events. For the older Deistical separation of God and nature, they substitute a God revealing Himself *in* the natural order—an 'immanence' of God in nature—in Carlyle's phrase, a 'natural supernaturalism.'[1] Like Goethe, they ask: 'What were a God who only gave the world a push from without, or let it spin round His finger?' and with the same author they reply: 'It is fitting for Him to move the world from within, to foster nature in Himself, Himself in nature; so that, whatever lives and moves and has its being in Him never lacks His power or His Spirit.'[2] Here then, and not in interruptions of the orderly course of things in nature, is laid, it is held, the surest, and at the same time the broadest and worthiest foundation of a doctrine of revelation. No other, it is claimed, is needed; for who can doubt that a God immanent and active in every thought and impulse of the human mind, and teaching and disciplining hourly by the events of life, can, even if the old-world belief in miracle be granted to be baseless, secure that everything needed for the welfare, guidance and inspiration of the race is furnished to it?

2. The side of truth represented in the view now sketched, one-sided as it is when taken by itself, should not be inconsiderately passed over. One of the spiritual gains of the last century was undoubtedly the fall of the older Deistic conception

[1] *Sartor Resartus*, bk. III. chap. viii.
[2] Quoted by Pfleiderer, *Giff. Lects.* i. p. 288.

referred to—never, however, that of true Christian theology—which separated God from His universe, and the replacement of this by the idea of an *immanent* relation of God to the world, and to the human spirit; not necessarily, indeed, to the denial of a *transcendent* relation as well, which is the opposite error, but as imposing on the mind the need of thinking of God's relation to the world as not outward and mechanical, but as inward and vital. This change had naturally its effect on the idea of revelation, which came also to be apprehended in a more vital way. A right philosophy teaches us to recognise an element of God's self-revelation in every true thought, every worthy exercise of faculty, every achievement of genius, every advance in knowledge and discovery. The essential difference of standpoint on the subject lies, not in disputing God's presence and self-revelation in nature, but in the point of whether this is to be regarded as *all*—whether, as God's supernatural *Being* transcends nature, so His supernatural *action* also, in the process of revelation, may not transcend the necessitated order of causes and effects, and manifest itself in extraordinary, because free and personal ways.

In view of this divergence of opinion on the subject of the supernatural, the attempt may now be made to define more exactly the different attitudes taken up at the present time to the idea of revelation.

III. (*A.*) THE RELIGIOUS-NATURALISTIC TENDENCY.

A first place must be given to the view just indicated—that which *identifies* the natural and the supernatural. Though claimed as distinctively 'modern,' it must not be supposed that the view in question is really new. Goethe and Carlyle have been quoted. But the doctrine has been the favourite one of humanists, philosophers, and the higher class of speculative thinkers from the beginning; has been familiar since the days of Spinoza, Lessing, and Herder. For a classical illustration, it is not necessary to go beyond Schleiermacher. To this thinker, in his *Discourses on Religion*, every intuition or original feeling is a 'revelation'; 'inspiration' is simply the general expression for the feeling of true morality and freedom; 'prophecy' is the religious anticipation of the other half of a religious event, one half being given,[1] and so on.

1. There can be no question, in any case, that the obliteration of the *distinction* of 'natural' and 'supernatural' in revelation, as in the other spheres of God's action, is the watchword of much of our modern thinking. In the general theory of revelation, its result is the identification of the revealing process with the ordinary psychological activities, and the refusal to admit any higher, distinctively supernatural, action of the Holy Spirit, in guiding into or imparting truth. As an influential theologian of the past generation, Biedermann of Zurich, succinctly put the point: 'The division of revelation into *natural* and *supernatural* is ambiguous in expression and abstract and figurative as respects the fact. It opposes as two *kinds* of

[1] *Reden*, ii. (*Werke*, i. pp. 249-50). On Schleiermacher's more mature view of revelation in his *Der Christ. Glaube*, see Dorner, *Syst. of Doct.* ii. pp. 157-8.

revelation what are only two *moments* of all revelation, inseparable from one another. All revelation is essentially *supernatural*, if under nature is understood the natural determinateness of man as finite, in opposition to his spiritual destination; and all revelation is just as essentially *natural*, if under nature is understood what belongs to his essence.'[1]

2. In the treatment of Scripture the effects of this anti-supernaturalistic tendency are seen in the complete *elimination* of the miraculous element in both Old Testament and New, save, indeed, as any seeming wonder (*e.g.*, bodily healings) can be naturally explained, and in the expunging, or explaining away, of all genuine prediction in prophecy. How extensively this principle rules in recent criticism no one acquainted with the book and magazine literature of our time needs to be informed. Kuenen's often-quoted remark on the religion of Israel in its relation to other religions stands for the position of a whole school. 'For us,' he says, 'the religion of Israel is one of these religions; nothing less, but also nothing more.'[2] Gunkel was cited above on Israel as 'the people of revelation.' Yet he says expressly, 'The history of revelation is transacted among men according to the same psychological laws as every other human event.'[3] Wellhausen, Duhm, Stade, Cornill, with their numerous followers in other countries, are here agreed. 'God,' says Cornill, 'who always and everywhere reveals Himself and works in history, has also revealed Himself and worked in the same way in history's greatest and most significant phase,

[1] *Christ. Dogmatik*, i. p. 265.
[2] *Rel. of Israel*, i. p. 5.
[3] *Op. cit.* p. 37.

the history of Israel's religion'; adding in defence: 'The natural and the naturalistic are of two kinds; would it be really unworthy of God if the process could be shown to proceed naturally? Is it not just the natural that is the greatest marvel?'[1] The like conception is applied by Bousset, Wernle, Loisy, and the school they represent, to the life of Jesus and the origins of Christianity, with like result in the elimination of all miracle.

3. The large assumption underlying this denial of a direct supernatural factor in revelation, viz., the *unbroken continuity* of nature, and consequent impossibility of the miraculous, falls to be discussed at a later stage. The assumption itself, given forth with confidence as a self-evident postulate of the modern mind, recurs so constantly that special illustration is hardly necessary. As a recent example, it may suffice to quote the statement in an able work on *The Philosophical Basis of Religion* by Professor John Watson, of Queen's University, Kingston, Canada:—

'Moreover,' this writer says, 'the Christianity of our day must be consistent with the highest products of reflection. We cannot now adopt in reference to it a view of history which has been exploded in other spheres; we cannot believe that there are cataclysms in the realm of spirit any more than in the realm of nature. There are no breaks in the life of humanity any more than in the external world. Therefore the kingdom of heaven must consist in the development of goodness in and through the ordinary processes by which man is ever realising his ideals. . . . Hence, just as there was a

[1] *Introd. to O. T.* (E.T.), p. 116.

primitive view of history and of nature, so there is a modern view which Christianity must incorporate on pain of extinction.' [1]

It might be truer to say that the Christianity which incorporates this 'modern' view is, not *threatened* with extinction, but is already extinguished.

IV. (*B.*) The Critical-Supernaturalistic Tendency.

It is now, however, time to point out that, with all its claims to be the sole representative of the 'modern' spirit, this naturalistic school has by no means the whole field to itself; that, on the contrary, its fundamental contention is widely dissented from, even among those who go far with it in its general critical attitude to Scripture—at least to the Old Testament. There is a *believing-critical*, as well as a naturalistic school of thinkers, and their opinions also need to be taken account of.

1. Superficial parallels have often been drawn between the Jewish and Christian Scriptures and the sacred books of other religions. But the impartial mind cannot ignore the fact that in the writings which constitute our Bible there is a unity and progression, a guiding purpose, culminating in Jesus Christ and His redemption, a fulness and

[1] *Op. cit.* p. 187. Cf. Bousset: 'Corresponding to modern culture, there is a special mode of thinking which is essentially peculiar to it. The main characteristic of this modern mode of thinking rests upon the determination to try to explain everything that takes place in the world by natural causes: or—to express it in another form—it rests on the determined assertion of universal laws to which all phenomena, natural and spiritual, are subject' (*Op. cit.* p. 283).

power of religious truth, which place them in a category by themselves, and compel the acknowledgment of a unique origin answering to their unique character. There have never been wanting in the critical schools men able to perceive this. It is important constantly to remember, and fair to recognise, that, if much unsettlement has resulted from the modern critical movement, in its bearings on the ideas of revelation and inspiration, the unsettlement has not been without many positive compensations. Dr. Sanday has truly remarked that we have witnessed about the utmost lengths to which the critical movement can go. 'It is impossible,' he says, 'for any theory started in the future to be more thoroughly naturalistic than many of those which we already have before us.' [1] But the movement has not been wholly destructive. It will be enough at present to mention one important gain: the demonstration, viz., which the application of the strictest historical and critical methods has afforded of the absolutely unique and extraordinary character of the religion of Israel. As the present writer has urged elsewhere,[2] with the best will in the world to explain the religious development of Israel by principles applicable to all religions, the efforts of the critics have resulted in a magnificent demonstration of the immense and unaccountable difference between the religion of this people and every other. The difference is independent of theories of the age of books, and impresses the mind nearly as strongly on the newer view of Israel's development as on the older. How is it to be

[1] *Inspiration*, p. 2.
[2] *The Problem of the Old Testament*, p. 10.

explained? Can psychological causes alone account for it? They can not. The further inquiry has gone, the tendency has increasingly been to force from the lips of the critics themselves the word 'revelation.'

2. It will not be doubted, at least, that this distinctive character of the Biblical revelation is upheld by the greater number of our best known British critical scholars, *e.g.*, by Dr. Driver, Dr. Sanday, the late Dr. A. B. Davidson, Dr. G. A. Smith, and others. The same is true of a multitude of Old Testament and New Testament critical scholars on the Continent, yet surely without the forfeiture thereby of their right to the title 'modern,' so calmly appropriated by the other side to itself. Here, as before, a few examples may suffice.

The facts which weigh chiefly with these critical writers in determining their admission of a supernatural origin of the religion of the Old Testament—*a fortiori* of that of the New—are such as these: the spiritual and ethical character of the Old Testament monotheism—its idea of God; the organic unity of the history and religion; the evidence throughout of a divine redemptive purpose, reaching its goal in Jesus Christ; not least, the overmastering impression of Hebrew prophecy. All these points of view are strikingly represented in a lecture given a few years ago by Professor Kautzsch, of Halle, on *The Abiding Value of the Old Testament*. This distinguished scholar emphasises the ethical and religious significance of the Old Testament. It is, he contends, inexhaustible, because it springs from the root of faith in a living God of unconditioned holiness and righteousness, who is at the same time a God of redeeming grace. 'The abiding value of the Old Testament lies above all in this, that it guarantees to us with absolute certainty the fact and the process of a divine plan and way of salvation, which found its conclusion and fulfilment in the New Covenant, in the Person and work of Jesus Christ.' 'Every attempt,' he declares, 'at explanation through human reflection or natural development, every form, in short, of evolutionary theory, now in such high favour, shatters on one fact—that of prophecy.' The distinguishing mark by which prophecy is raised high as heaven above all heathen phenomena with which it may be compared is, that it 'stands in the service of a divine plan of salvation.' The prophets are living witnesses to, and guarantee, the fact that there is direct communication between God and man.[1]

Similarly, the development of God's redemptive 'plan' was held by the late Professor Dillmann to be the central idea of the Old Testament;[2] and Professor Kittel, a disciple of Dillmann's, writes in his *History of the Hebrews*: 'Nothing but an immediate contact of God Himself with man can produce the true knowledge of God, or bring man a real step nearer thereto'; while, of 'the new and lofty knowledge of God possessed by Moses,' he declares: 'That knowledge came neither from his age nor from himself; it came to him from the immediate revelation of God in his heart.'[3]

Professor G. A. Smith, in his *Modern Criticism and the Preaching of the Old Testament*, bases his 'Proof of

[1] *Op. cit.* pp. 22, 24, 28-9, 30-1.
[2] Cf. Dillmann, *Alttest. Theol.* p. 441.
[3] *Op. cit.* i. (E.T.) p. 252.

a Divine Revelation in the Old Testament' on the fact that, 'in a physical environment, very fertile in polytheism,' Israel alone was enabled, 'not merely to rise above this to a stage of religion subordinate only to the Christianity of Christ, but to exhibit throughout her whole history a religious progress which Christ affirmed to be the gradual preparation for Himself'; and says: 'To this unique exception in the history of Semitic religion it is my firm belief that only one cause can be assigned, and that is, that in the religion of Israel, as recorded in the Old Testament, there was an authentic revelation of the one true God.' [1]

3. Naturally, in light of these facts, prominence is given to the idea of 'organic unity' in the Biblical religion as a mark of its origin in revelation. Apart from all theories about the Bible, the earnest student cannot but be struck by observing in how marked a degree it is a structural unity—has a beginning, a middle, and an end. The Bible is a unique book in this respect, however, only because it is the record of a unique revelation. It is in the religion, the revelation, that the real mystery and wonder lie. It is there, in God's progressive self-revelation, that the organic unity which impresses the mind so strongly is to be sought for. Hence, a writer like H. Schultz, in speaking of the religion of Israel, can observe that it is 'not a variety of forms of religion which have merely an outward connection of space and time,' which has to be dealt with, 'but *one* religion, though distinct stages of its development, which, consequently, are dynamically and inwardly bound together'; in

[1] *Op. cit.* p. 126.

the representation of which 'each member must hark back on the preceding, a common thread of living tissue must bind all together—the representation must be, not merely "historical," but "genetic."'[1]

A like organic unity, combined with progressive development, it might be shown, reveals itself in *doctrine*. While throwing off, or suffering to fall into the background, what is accidental or temporary, each stage in the advance of revelation takes up what is vital and permanent in the preceding stage. No single grain of the word of God 'which liveth and abideth'[2] is allowed to perish in the process.

V. (*C.*) The Evangelical-Positive Tendency.

1. The above testimonies, chosen from writers of critical repute, show conclusively that faith in a supernatural revelation is not only not subverted, but in certain respects, and for certain minds, is directly aided by the view of the Scriptures usually denominated 'critical.' This the adherents of a yet stricter view of revelation and inspiration—what, for distinction's sake, may be called the *evangelical-positive*—will freely grant. These feel, at the same time, that, in other respects, the extreme lengths to which critical theories are frequently carried—the manner in which critics take the Bible to pieces and dissect its text, the free fashion in which they impugn its historical credibility, the later dates they assign to its narratives, and the extensive place they allow to myth, legend, invention—in numerous instances, to intentional fraud,—create serious difficulties in carrying through a consistent

[1] *O. T. Theol.* (E.T.) i. p. 3. [2] 1 Pet. i. 23.

doctrine of revelation and inspiration, and are, in no small degree, responsible for the existing widely-spread unsettlement of opinion on these subjects. The learned Dr. Dorner, in the sections on 'Revelation' in his *System of Doctrine*[1]—sections marked by his accustomed profundity and insight —may be named as an earlier representative of this more conservative position. It is, despite the 'modern' current that has set in, probably, in essential idea, the position of the great majority of evangelical Christians still. A few words, therefore, may be said in its elucidation.

2. Criticism has to do with the external form of the Scriptures, and those are at all times few who are capable of entering into the intricacies of critical argument. There is something, however, deeper than external form, on which it is possible for the humblest to form a judgment, and which will surely carry the student of divine revelation further into the heart of the subject than any amount of critical learning would do—by neglect of which, in truth, the ablest critics go continually astray. The one thing criticism can never expunge from this book, the Bible, is what we speak of as the *Gospel*—its continuous, coherent, self-attesting discovery to man of the mind of God regarding man himself, his sin, the guilt and ruin into which sin has plunged him, and over against that the method of a divine salvation, the outcome of a purpose of eternal love, wrought out in ages of progressive revelation, and culminating in the mission, life, death, atoning work, and resurrection of His Son Jesus Christ, and in the gift of His Spirit to the

[1] Vol. ii. pp. 133 ff.

Church and believers. Here also is a fact—the biggest and most solid fact in the universe—a fact patent on the face of Scripture to any one who reads with open eyes, intertwined with ages of Christian experience, with enduring institutions, with efforts and achievements, which furnish a continuous proof of its reality. So long as this fact stands, the Scriptures will also stand. For it is the Scriptures which, in their divers parts and divers manners, embody and convey to us this revelation of God, and by the verifiable presence of this revelation in them, the Scriptures are proved to be, what they claim to be, the living and inspired oracles of God.[1]

Here, then, it is, in the evangelical view, within Scripture, not outside of it,—within this grand, cathedral-like structure of divine revelation,—within this massive, comprehensive, divinely-unique plan of God's salvation for a world of sinners,—that the believer in revelation must take his stand, if he is to recover lost ground in regard to the Scriptures. He is here at the heart—the centre—not at the circumference. In the light of what he beholds of the realised saving purpose of God in the New Testament, he looks back upon the stages of its development in the Old, and feels the ground there also firm beneath his feet. Criticism does not make him anxious, for he knows that excesses of criticism must always be blocked and checked by the presence of this vital evangelical element which

[1] 2 Tim. iii. 15-17. The above statements are made with clear recognition that it is precisely these evangelical doctrines which, in the 'modern view' of Christianity, are swept away (cf. Bousset, *Op. cit.* p. 292, and see below, p. 33).

runs continuously throughout Scripture. If he is told, as he will be, that he is beginning at the wrong end,—that he has first to prove that the Bible is God's Word, and only then can go on to speak of its Gospel,—his reply is the simple one, that it is the fact that the Bible has this Gospel in the heart of it which, above all else, proves to him that it *is* God's Word. If that Gospel is in the Bible, he is as sure as he is of his own existence that it was not man who put it there. It is too high for him; he could not attain to it. The Bible reveals man to himself as he could never have known himself without its help. It reveals God to him in lights and aspects of His grace which it could never have entered the wildest dreams of his imagination to conceive. It embodies that grace in a divine plan, working itself out in an extended history, which it is absolutely certain no sinful mind could have invented. A book which contains such a Gospel needs no external attestation to prove that God speaks through it with authority to men.

3. The idea of revelation reached along this line is obviously much more definite in character than any conception obtained by more general methods. It has also a *regulative* value which other views have not. Accepting a supernatural economy of grace as the central fact of revelation, it is not trammelled by the *a priori* presumptions about miracle which are apt to vitiate purely critical theories. For miracle is of the very essence of the economy. It is able to take up firmer ground on historicity; for it sees the meaning and place of the great facts in the Biblical history, as other theories do not. It recognises a line of divine revelation extending

through all time. It is therefore prepared to accept the fact of a record of such special, continuous, supernatural revelation.

VI. Advances in Later Thought.

It is still, however, to be acknowledged that, even within the limits of this—the stricter and more positive school on the subject of revelation and inspiration — considerable *changes* and in some respects *advances*, have taken place, due to the widened outlook and more scientific temper of the age. These will come up in the general course of the discussion, and need only be briefly glanced at here.

1. One chief advance is the clearer distinction made between *revelation* and *Holy Scripture*—a distinction for which much is owing to Rothe, one of the most suggestive writers on the doctrine of revelation. This distinction, as Rothe points out,[1] the older evangelical theology tended almost completely to ignore. Revelation in large part preceded its record; yet, as will be seen later, revelation and Scripture come to be *for us* practically synonymous and co-extensive.[2]

2. Another change is the clearer conception of revelation itself as something primarily *historical*. Instead of revelation being regarded as consisting simply or exclusively in the communication of truths or ideas through internal suggestion, illumination, or intuition—the *doctrinaire* view of revelation, as the late Professor A. B. Bruce called it—its essence is seen to lie, primarily, in a series of

[1] Cf. his *Zur Dogmatik*, pp. 54-5. [2] See below, p. 59.

divine *acts*: 'God manifesting Himself in the history of the world in a supernatural manner and for a special purpose.'[1] This, of course, is not intended as the denial of *subjective* and *internal* revelation, as in prophets and apostles. It is still an important advance when, in accordance with the Biblical conception itself, the stress is shifted back, even from prophetic and apostolic teaching, to the divine acts which stand behind both. 'He made known His ways unto Moses, His doings unto the children of Israel.'[2] God's saving acts in Israel—His dealings in grace with the nation and its fathers—stood behind the prophets' message, and formed the basis of their knowledge of God and confidence in Him. Similarly, the work of the apostles stands in a subsidiary, interpretative, and ministrative relation to the historical revelation of God in the personal manifestation of Christ.

3. A third gain in the modern treatment lies in a more *dynamical* view of inspiration, as distinguished from a theory of mechanical dictation—an idea sometimes confounded with that of inspiration, but now hardly defended by any school.[3] Both revelation and inspiration are conceived of, without prejudice to their supernatural origin, as standing in the closest relation to the capacity,

[1] Bruce, *Chief End of Revelation*, p. 57. Dr. Bruce closely follows Rothe on this point.

[2] Ps. ciii. 7.

[3] Recent writers of all schools allow the fullest play in inspiration to the *individuality* of the sacred writers. See, among conservative writers, Lee, *Inspiration of Holy Scripture*, pp. 361 ff.; Bannerman, *Inspiration of the Scriptures*, pp. 453 ff.; Hodge and Warfield, art. 'Inspiration' in *The Presbyterian Review*, April 1881. To this last important article a good many references will be made.

experience, and mental endowments of the individual, and to the circumstances of his age. Connected with this is to be observed an *enlargement* of the idea of inspiration to include, or at least take account of, the *entire process* by which, under the providential superintendence of God, and guidance of His Spirit, the inspired record has been produced.[1] Special stress is laid on the intimate relations of 'inspiration' and 'providence.'[2] The importance of this conjunction will be afterwards seen.[3]

4. Probably, however, the principal advance in the modern handling of this subject is in the attempts at the more accurate discrimination of the related ideas of *revelation* and *inspiration* themselves. So long as revelation was directly identified with Scripture, such discrimination was impossible; now nearly all writers recognise a distinction between the two ideas.[4] It is to be acknowledged, nevertheless, that much haziness still rests over this whole part of the inquiry, and that, in the distinction of the relations of revelation and inspiration, too much has occasionally been looked for from mere verbal refinements. The distinctions offered are far from

1 Thus, in the Gospels, there is the personal ministry of Jesus, the oral teaching and preaching of the apostles, leading to the segregation and formation into an oral type of the incidents and sayings of Jesus which formed the synoptic tradition, the earlier records of parts of this tradition, which may have entered into the composition of the Gospels, etc. An element of inspiration and divine guidance is present through the whole. (Cf. Westcott, *Introduction to the Study of the Gospels*, pp. 28, 32, 166, etc.)

2 Westcott, as above; Hodge and Warfield in article cited. The inter-connection of inspiration and providence may be said to be the thesis of this article.

3 See below, p. 213.

4 The writers above quoted all do so, and most others.

agreeing among themselves, and in all their forms seem open to manifest objections. A few examples may be given.

According to Rothe, *manifestation*, which is the external and objective side of revelation, and *inspiration*, which is its internal and subjective side, combine in inseparable unity to constitute the actual *revelation*. But revelation, it is plain, is sometimes wholly internal.[1]

According to Dr. Lee, *revelation* has reference to a supernatural communication of knowledge from God to man: *inspiration* is 'that actuating energy of the Holy Spirit . . . guided by which the human agents chosen by God have *officially* proclaimed His will by word of mouth, or have committed to writing the several portions of the Bible. . . . Revelation and inspiration are also to be distinguished by the sources from which they proceed, revelation being the peculiar function of the eternal Word; inspiration the result of the agency of the Holy Spirit.'[2] Does the Spirit then not reveal? The idea of revelation here, besides, is too exclusively *doctrinal*.

Dr. A. M. Fairbairn propounds a view which is nearly the reverse of this. 'God inspires, man reveals. Inspiration is the process by which God gives; revelation is the mode or form—word, character, or institution—in which man embodies that which he has received. The words, though not equivalent, are co-extensive, the one denoting the process on its inner side, the other on its outer.'[3]

[1] *Op. cit.* pp. 68-9.

[2] *Op. cit.* pp. 27-29.

[3] *Christ in Mod. Theol.* p. 496. For other statements of the distinction, see Dorner, as above; Ladd, *Doct. of Scripture*, i. p. 321; Bannerman, *Op. cit.* p. 151; Westcott, *Op. cit.* p. 8, etc.

The subject will be considered later, but here it may provisionally be asked: Can there be any form of internal revelation (*e.g.*, prophetic) which does not imply as its condition and correlate an exalted or 'inspired' state of soul? Or can there be any inspiration which is not attended by a measure of 'revelation'—of insight into divine things? If not, are not the two ideas inseparably conjoined? On its objective side, again, has not 'revelation' a much more extended range than is sometimes given to it? Who, *e.g.*, can fail to see that, in the Old Testament, revelation is not confined to the specifically miraculous acts or words of God, but includes the whole historical dealing of God with Israel, and the providential relations of that people with other nations (Egypt, Assyria, Chaldæa)—in other words, carries us beyond the distinctively miraculous into the sphere of God's ordinary providence? The important fact becomes apparent that it is not always or only in the *means* or *method* of God's working, so much as in the *result*,[1] that we are to look for the qualities of divine revelation.

[1] Cf. Hodge and Warfield, as above.

CHAPTER II

NATURALISTIC SCHEMES OF REVELATION—SCOPE AND LIMITS OF NATURAL REVELATION

It has been seen in the previous chapter that God and revelation are correlative ideas. Revelation is 'unveiling,' and divine revelation is God's unveiling of the truth regarding Himself in some manner and degree to the intelligence and heart of man. Only as He does thus unveil Himself does He become known to man. It is futile, therefore, to set to work to prove the being, personality and character of God before studying the nature and modes of His self-revelation. Only in studying the revelation do we get to know the God who reveals.

I. Nature *versus* Revelation.

The statement just made, that, if there is not a living, personal God, there can be no proper 'revelation,' might seem evident from the very force of the terms. If nature be self-sufficient and self-explaining, the all and sole Reality, there can be no revelation of aught beyond itself. There are those, however, who dispute this, and plead that nothing more than nature is necessary as a basis for religion. Nature is its own revelation. The infinite mystery and wonder of the universe constitute it, on their view, a sufficient object of reverence. For 'God' is substituted 'the All,' 'the Universum,' 'Nature'; and religion, identified with 'cosmic emotion,' becomes worship at the altar of the Unknowable.[1] Or the Pantheism latent in such expressions may become explicit, and God be spoken of as the Eternal Power, Spirit, Energy, which reveals or discovers itself in outward appearances. So long, however, as the idea of revelation is arrested at this stage,—so long as the process of manifestation is regarded as a necessary one, be the necessity physical, or be it logical,—revelation in the proper sense cannot be spoken of. The only idea of God which answers to the idea of revelation is that of a Being who has character and will—power to reveal, and purpose and end in revealing,—who is self-conscious personal, and ethical.[2]

II. Natural Revelation—How to be Conceived.

It must be left to the course of the discussion to justify the assumption that this is truly the nature of the Being who has become known to us through the various modes of His self-revelation. It is the *manner* of this self-revelation which is now to be considered. And a first question relates to the place to be accorded to *Natural Revelation*.

1. A distinction made by Ewald in his treatment

1 Cf. Strauss's *Der alte und der neue Glaube*; Seeley's *Natural Religion*, and similar works. For a good criticism, see Bruce, *The Miraculous Elements in the Gospels*, pp. 378 ff.

2 Even Mr. Spencer speaks of the Power manifested in evolution as in some sense self-revealing. He speaks of 'the naturally-revealed end towards which the Power manifested throughout evolution works' (*Data of Ethics*, p. 171). Cf. a striking passage in his *First Principles*, p. 123.

of revelation may furnish us with a starting-point.[1] Ewald begins his discussion of this subject by distinguishing between what he calls *immediate* and *mediate* revelation. The 'immediate' revelation, in his view, is without a sufficiently clear and perfectly sure word, and embraces the original revelation given in the human spirit in creation, the creation itself as it stands in its glory and perfection before the gaze of man's spirit, and the whole history of the human race, which to the prepared mind teaches truths of eternal freshness and force. 'Mediate' revelation, which alone, he says, deserves the name revelation in the fullest sense, expresses itself, on the other hand, in intelligible and distinct words. It is the word of God through human discourse. The word of God thus mediated is declared to have a truly supernatural source, and to stand in connection with definite historical occasions. The obvious criticism to be made on this distinction, in many ways suggestive, is, that the natural revelation is also in a true sense 'mediate,'—is mediated by the whole system and course of things through which it comes,—and that the higher or supernatural revelation, assuming such to exist, is not always or only, as indeed Ewald himself recognises, through human discourse, but is primarily, as before indicated, through *acts* or *deeds* of God—through divine *facts* which human speech interprets or conveys.

The distinction which Ewald has in view is better reached by speaking simply, as is more usual, of *general* and *special*, or of *natural* and *supernatural*

[1] Cf. his *Revelation: its Nature and Record* (E. T. of first volume of his *Die Lehre der Bibel von Gott*), pp. 5 ff.

revelation. The former is perhaps the preferable expression, if only for the reason already given, that *all* revelation, even when mediated through only natural means, is supernatural, in the sense that it has a supernatural basis, and that it is supernatural truth that is revealed.

2. The reality of a natural revelation of God is everywhere assumed in Scripture,[1] and in some sense has generally been conceded by serious minds. Yet *the attitudes taken up* to this natural revelation at different periods, and by different schools of thinkers, have greatly varied. In Christian circles there has usually been the attempt to do justice to all the truth about God made known through natural means, while upholding the need and reality of revelation of a higher and more special kind for the guidance of man into the full knowledge of God's character and will, and for the ends of man's redemption. This balance of view, however, it is difficult rightly to maintain; and frequently, in the history of religious thought, the opposite tendencies have been witnessed, on the one hand, to the *over-exaltation* of the natural revelation, on the other, to its undue *belittlement*.

(1) The eighteenth century may be said to be the period, *par excellence*, of the exaltation of the powers of reason, and the assertion of the *all-sufficiency* of natural revelation. The Deism of that century had for its aim to exhibit the revelation of God in nature as yielding a few simple, unchanging truths about God, virtue, immortality, and future recompense—those truths of which all positive religions,

[1] *E.g.* Pss. viii.; xix. 1-5; cxix. 89-91; Is. xl. 12-14, 26; Acts xiv. 15-17; Rom. i. 19, 20.

with their priestcrafts, were the corruptions—and this in so clear a manner as to render superfluous all special or miraculous revelation. This Deistical phase passed with the assaults of a sceptical and critical philosophy on its foundations, and with the recognition that there never had been, nor could be, any such universal 'natural religion'; that what was put forth as such was simply a colourless abstract of truths borrowed from the positive religions, and especially from Christianity—truths which, separated from their vital roots in these religions, had no emotional or spiritual value.

(2) It is not surprising that, in recoil from a lifeless Deism and a speculative rationalism, the opposite tendency has sometimes been manifested to do *less* than justice to the natural revelation. More recently, this tendency is specially apparent in the German Ritschlian school, which, on the ground of a theoretic Agnosticism derived from Kant, and a theory of religion which seeks in the help of superior powers deliverance from the thwarting influences of man's natural environment, would expel 'natural theology' altogether from Christianity, and rest everything on the 'revelation-value' of the Person of Jesus Christ. It is not denied by Ritschl and his followers that in some sense there is 'revelation' also in the lower stages of religion. But it is not the kind of revelation which the ordinary 'natural theology' supposes, and, whatever its worth for its immediate recipients, it is viewed as now left behind, and valueless for Christians.[1]

(3) This, however, is too obviously an exaggeration to find general acceptance. Once more, accordingly,

[1] Cf. Herrmann, *Op. cit.* pp. 49, 50, 53-4.

the wheel has turned, and partly as a development from Ritschlianism itself, partly as a result of wider tendencies in the culture of the age, a *new 'religious-historical'* school has arisen, which, merging Christianity in the general stream of religious development, and again universalising the idea of revelation, includes all religions equally as phases of this development. Agreeing with Deism and speculative rationalism in the rejection of supernatural revelation, this school differs from the former in renouncing the abstract point of view, and attaching itself to the idea of the historical evolution of religion, and from the latter in seeking the origin of religion in practical impulses, and refusing to regard it as simply the vehicle of rational and moral ideas. As it is this school which is at present coming to the front, it is desirable to give it closer attention.

III. Bousset on Religion and Revelation.

It will help to the comprehension of the positions of the 'religious-historical' school if a single book be accepted for guidance, and for this purpose a better aid could not be desired than is afforded by Professor W. Bousset's recently-published work, *What is Religion?*

Here, to begin with, are a few sentences from this book on the general standpoint:

'History would appear to destroy the idea of inspiration—that is to say, of any special revelation—in the Old and New Testament. . . . And what if history were right? Suppose this view were the true one? In that case only a bold step forward will save us. If the science of history demands that the seals be broken, and the special revelation be surrendered, then we must seriously consider the idea of a universal revelation.' [1]

Earlier: 'It is no question of *This* religion is true; *that* is false; everywhere we perceive growth, evolution, imperfection striving towards perfection. . . . The whole history of the religious life of mankind stands to us as the great handiwork of God, a ceaseless apparition and constant intercourse of God with man, of man with his Maker, in accordance with the stage to which he has attained.' [2]

The theme of the book is then developed thus. In accordance with his standpoint, Bousset first explains *what religion is*—desire for life, belief in gods or a god, surrender and sacrifice, longing for redemption;—and *how it originates*—in man's sense of wonder ('on the boundary-line between the known and the Unknown' [3]), and in the animistic principle moving the savage to people nature with innumerable spirits and ghosts of the dead. Religion is next traced in its *evolution* from the fetishism, magic, and worship of the dead of savages, through tribal religion, with its idea of blood-relationship, and its loftier objects of worship ('in the tribal life reverence for common gods or for one universal God predominates' [4]), and national religions, as in Babylonia, Egypt, and Greece, with their developed polytheisms, to the prophetic stage. This stage, held to be more monotheistic in character, with a

[1] Pp. 289-90 (E. T.). Cf. Sabatier, *Outlines of a Phil. of Rel.* (E. T.), p. 34: 'I conceive therefore that revelation is as universal as religion itself, that it descends as low, goes as far, ascends as high, and accompanies it always.'

[2] P. 9. [3] Pp. 18, 20. [4] P. 58.

retrocession to religions of the law ('in the history of religion the valleys succeed the heights'[1]), is represented by Zarathustra, Buddha, and Confucius, by Socrates and Plato in Greece, above all by the prophets of Israel. Finally, from the prophetic impulse proceed 'religions of redemption' (Buddhism, Platonism), and, as the highest of these, Christianity. The religion of Jesus, with its spiritual view of God, its freedom from nationality and ceremonial, its moral aim, and its proclamation of redemption ('Christianity is the religion of moral redemption, and its highest good is the forgiveness of sin and guilt, and the freeing of the will towards the good'[2]), is that which, 'if there is to be only one religion, must be the religion of the progressive nations of the earth.'[3]

It is carefully to be observed, however, where Christianity is spoken of, that, in our author's view, *the Christianity of the future* is to be a Christianity completely purified from all its ordinarily accepted supernatural elements. The 'Pauline-Lutheran' conception of Christianity, it is declared, 'cannot any longer be accepted in modern life, with its absolutely independent attitude.'[4] 'All is here based on the opposition between sin and grace, and in the centre of religion is placed the consciousness of sin, and the consolation of freedom from sin and guilt.'[5] Such a conception, it is said, cannot stand. 'We can no longer speak of the "divinity" of Christ.'[6] 'The belief in the special significance of Christ's sacrificial death' is repudiated by our moral consciousness.[7] Human corruption cannot be

[1] P. 136. [2] Pp. 267-8. [3] P. 269. [4] P. 277.
[5] P. 276. [6] P. 279. [7] P. 281.

preached.[1] Miracles, of course, have no place in the new scheme.[2] 'Christianity, in its essential idea, dominant up to the present, is based on a fundamental conception utterly opposed to the ideal of life which has just been described. The narrow Pauline idea of redemption, which was developed by St. Augustine, and strengthened anew by Luther, still dominates it.'[3] This must be parted with. 'If we accept in its entirety this conception, if, that is, we take from modern life its very essence, and force it to self-renunciation, we shall have absolutely to cast on one side such complete and great figures as those of Goethe and Bismarck.'[4] This last consideration, naturally, is, with the author, final.

IV. Criticism of Bousset's Theory.

With full acknowledgment of the many interesting side-lights thrown on the history of religion by Bousset's book, the general criticism which suggests itself on the scheme unfolded in it may be very simply stated. It is *not* historical; it does not do justice to the true idea of religion, and at every stage hopelessly mixes up things that differ; it negates the true conception of revelation, and removes from Christianity the elements which alone give it vitality, and enable it to do the work required of it. In an important sense, its end contradicts its beginning. This general judgment it is now necessary to justify.

1. The scheme professes to be *evolutionary*. Evolution, however, in the right conception of it, is a process in which *one continuous life* is seen

[1] P. 278. [2] P. 284. [3] P. 275. [4] Pp. 274, 276-7.

unfolding itself; in which one stage is seen emerging from another, to give place, in turn, to a higher stage. It is not a true historical evolution when, as here, different types of religion, higher and lower grades of social existence, in different parts of the world, are set in order of succession, with no attempt at proof that one has really grown from the other, or stands in any genetic relation to the other. It would be to the purpose if, following up the history of any one race or people, it were shown that it had passed by internal development through the stages indicated, or that, at least, the gains of one people had been appropriated by another, and there carried up to something higher.

(1) This, however, is precisely what is not done. Savage races are described (Polynesian, Indian, Mongolian, Negro, etc.)—fetishist, unprogressive, without chronology, incapable of fixed tribal union (though some of them are shown to have a highly developed tribal life[1]). But proof is lacking of any such race or tribe having emerged historically from that condition by self-development, without contact with a higher civilisation. National religions are depicted; but it is not shown that the higher elements in the Babylonian, Egyptian, Greek, or Vedic religions, were historically developed out of the fetishism, animism, ghost-worship, or totemism, of the savage state, or were preceded by them; still less that these polytheistic religions became simpler, purer, or more monotheistic in the course of their development, instead of becoming, as is historically the case, constantly more idolatrous, superstitious, and corrupt. Prophecy is treated

[1] Pp. 55-6.

as a stage in religious evolution; but it fails to be shown that prophecy in Israel—that unique phenomenon—had really any analogy to Buddhism or Platonism, or sprang from like causes, or that an outcome like Christianity was the product of development in any other people or religion but that of Israel.

(2) It has, in short, to be shown that *the higher elements* in the historical religions *are evolved out of the lower*, and this is not done and cannot be done. The spirit-worship, magic, ancestor-worship, etc., which is so common a feature among savages subsists as a lower stratum also in higher religions; but it is not shown that the higher is a development out of it. On the contrary, it is inconsequently allowed that the lower races which cherish these superstitions have also the idea of a supreme God, though they do not ordinarily worship Him;[1] that 'in the tribal life reverence for common gods or for one universal God predominates';[2] and that 'most widespread of all is the worship of the heavenly God—that is, of Heaven itself—which is not regarded as consisting of the many powers mentioned above, but as a single, powerful being. . . . The well-known

[1] 'Most of the Negro races recognise a powerful heavenly being, or god, that is to say, a giver of life, Heaven—not yet divided into different divine forms,' etc. . . . 'The same remark applies to the Malay-Polynesian race. An Almighty God is there recognised, etc. (p. 39). These races also regard it 'as a matter of course that in the human body there dwells an independent vital essence—the soul,' and that 'the soul never dies' (pp. 47-8). Side by side with such statements are the customary exaggerations, that 'the difference between man and animal is not felt,' 'the savage has no understanding of the connection of things,' 'uncivilised man does not yet know that the light of day proceeds from the sun,' etc. (pp. 33, 34, 59).

[2] P. 58.

similarity of names is clear evidence that the Indo-Germanic race before its separation into different tribes had a common possession in the worship of the God of heaven.'[1] When the national stage is reached, a new explanation is given of polytheism—with which is now connected image-worship—in the separate tribes which unite to form the nation bringing their tribal deities (assumed to be single) with them.[2] This polytheism becomes ever more firmly-rooted, intricate, and mythological. So far, in truth, from a spiritual monotheism being the natural outcome of this development, there are, as has often been remarked, even till this hour, only three monotheistic religions in the world—Judaism, Christianity, and Mohammedanism—and all three are derived from the Bible.

(3) The *ethical evolution* which the theory postulates is as little established as the religious. Is it true, for example, that in the Greek and Indian religions, 'the gods became the spiritual powers which, in accordance with eternal, inviolable laws, guide the destinies of the nations in holiness and righteousness?'[3] Or mark the blunting of ethical conceptions involved in such a conjunction of sentences as the following:—'The phenomenon of simple absorption in the Godhead now develops into horrible human sacrifice, especially in the form of sacrifice of children, and of prostitution' (illustrations are given from the Mexican religion, from sacrificing to Moloch, from Phoenicia, from prostitution in the service of the Canaanitish-Syrian Astarte, etc.). . . . 'Already we have wandered a good distance. Already we see that the religious life is striving after higher

[1] P. 60. [2] P. 71. [3] P. 20.

[!] forms, that a common faith is rising above the arbitrary thoughts and fantasies of the individual.' [1]

2. Viewed in its bearings on revelation, an evolutionary theory of this sort *does not universalise, but in reality excludes*, revelation proper. Bousset contends rightly that 'wherever we have religious life the gods (or the Godhead) are regarded as absolute realities, more real even than human life.' [2] Even he, however, will not argue that the fetishes, or multitudinous spirits of woods, hills, rivers, or the Baals, and Astartes, and Molochs, of tribal and national worship, *are* real beings, or aught but projections of the religious mind creating imaginary objects for itself.[3] It is not denied that a certain perception of the divine in nature—a true element of the natural revelation — may lie behind; but the embodiments of this perception are purely fanciful, products of a childish interpretation of nature, or something worse, horrible perversions of the idea of deity. The idea of the true God, when it comes, displaces these false conceptions, is not an evolution from them. Reality is not developed out of unreality. It is playing with words, for example, to treat the Yahweh of the Old Testament as at first a storm or wind god—an unreal being — created by man's own phantasy, then to regard this as the first stage in the revelation of the *real* Yahweh of the prophets—the living and true God— who chose Israel at the beginning to be His people.

3. This, finally, is what is meant by saying that

[1] P. 67. [2] P. 17.

[3] Contrasting these ideas with phenomena due to hypnotic suggestion, etc., Bousset himself speaks of them, apparently, as fantasies and products of the imagination (p. 46).

the end of the supposed evolutionary process *contradicts its beginning*. The culmination of the process is not even the God of the prophets, but is the God and Father of Jesus Christ—a holy God and heavenly Father, who loves His children, and is infinitely tender and pitiful toward them; whe surrounds them at every moment with His providential care, and seeks to bring them to the knowledge and love of Himself; who abhors and judges sin, yet is full of mercy to the returning sinner. Is it conceivable that such a God should have no means of access to the souls He has made other than that of evolutionary development? Or that He should choose as the only path by which man, through uncounted millenniums, should rise to the knowledge of Himself this tortuous way of sin, error, and vile and hideous practice? Or that this actually was the path by which man at length climbed to the consummate heights of the consciousness of Jesus Christ? Must we not in consistency, either alter our ideas of the method of revelation, or, retaining these, give up the conception of God attained through Christ at the end?

V. Sources of Natural Revelation.

Yet the *natural revelation remains*—in large part, as may be conceded to the Deist, unchanged from the creation; in another and wider respect, ceaselessly progressive, as man's own thoughts grow wider, as his knowledge of himself and of the natural universe increases, as the scroll of God's purposes is gradually unrolled in history. Ewald was right in speaking of this revelation as one both *within* and *without* man—as furnished in the very constitution of his own being, in the glory and order of the universe as it displays itself before him, and in the course of events of which he forms a part.

1. Analysing the sources of this revelation a little further, we distinguish the following :—

(1) First, there is the revelation *within* man, in man's own heart, from the beginning, in the sense of *dependence* on inscrutable powers, or on *a* Power, above and around him (one thinks here of Schleiermacher's 'feeling of absolute dependence,' or of the consciousness of the Absolute, taken by H. Spencer to be a constituent element in all experience) ; while, stirring within him, likewise from the beginning, is a rational spiritual nature, which will not let him rest till he has found an object adequate to his highest ideal—a God infinite, personal, ethical, and revealing. Later, as man comes reflectively to know himself, but still as part of this self-revelation of the divine, is the discovery made that God is the implicate of his entire rational and moral life,—the ultimate postulate of moral consciousness (Kant), of personal selfhood (Ritschl), of rational thought (Hegel). The whole distance is thus spanned between man's first, simplest, and most elementary sense of the divine, and the last conclusions of the profoundest philosophy of spirit. [1]

(2) But, next, over against man, the subject of religion, stands the *outer* revelation—that great, continual *manifestation* of God in the existence,

[1] The truth in such contentions as in Pfleiderer's *Gifford Lectures* or in Professor Watson's *Philosophical Basis of Religion* is here taken up. A sound philosophy must strive after a supreme unity which comprehends under itself the Ideas of the true and the good ; and this is the idea of God (Pfleiderer, i. p. 32).

stability, order, and manifold workings of His *natural creation*, in the events of man's life, and in his providential environment. The heavens and the earth declare the glory of their Creator. That which may be known of God, the Apostle says, is manifest through the things that are made—even His everlasting power and divinity.[1] God has not left Himself without witness, in that He did good, and gave from heaven rains and fruitful seasons. A revelation this, which antecedes all logical reasoning, which is universal, which is borne in on man insensibly, irresistibly, in all races and stages of culture, so long as any spark of spiritual susceptibility is left in him. There is no tribe or people, if the best investigations may be trusted, but manifests something of this 'sense of something far more deeply interfused'—this feeling of the infinite, as Schleiermacher and Max Müller would define it—this *sensus numinis* of the older writers,—which is the fact that lies behind the term 'Godhead,' and is involved in the attribution of 'divinity' to superior powers.[2]

(3) Yet, while this outward revelation is constant, and in its essential content unchanging, it, too, in the nature of the case, is endlessly *progressive*. How immensely, *e.g.*, has science, through the progress of discovery, enlarged man's thoughts of God in space and time, revolutionising, for it is nothing else, his whole idea of the cosmos! In how many ways has it illuminated God's methods of

[1] Rom. i. 20.

[2] The facts may be seen in such works as Max Müller's *Hibbert* and *Gifford Lectures*, Waitz's *Anthropologie* (Negro tribes), A. Lang's *The Making of Religion*, etc.

working, illustrating His power in things immeasurably great, and His care of things infinitely little, giving demonstration, in its extension throughout the universe of the reign of law, of His faithfulness; expanding also—though here there may be more demur—the conception of His goodness! For who can doubt, despite much that, to our imperfect vision, must create difficulty, and leaving out of view for the moment the evil and suffering for which man himself is responsible, that the optimist is right when he declares that the system of things is, on the whole, in its essential constitution and tendency, a beneficent one? The day may be regarded as past where such a conception as evolution was thought to conflict with, or supersede, the belief in ends, plan, purpose, intelligent ordering, and providential guidance, in creation. These ideas not simply stand secure; they have received firmer grounding in the best thought of evolutionary science itself.[1]

(4) The sources of the natural knowledge which man has, or may have, of God, are thus, as seen, both internal and external. It is now, lastly, to be remarked that these two sides of natural revelation, though separable in idea, are *not separable in fact*. The external world would reveal nothing of God without the key afforded by man's own rational and spiritual nature. The internal, again,—the world of personality, rationality, morality,—is evoked and developed only through contact and in interaction with the external. It is more, also, it should be observed, than an *idea* of God which man

[1] Cf. on this point R. Otto, *Naturalism and Religion* (E. T.), in 'Crown Theol. Library.'

reaches through these combined influences. In his own consciousness, and in the world around him, God is discovered to him as an actually existing Being—a Reality—an all-encompassing Presence—immeasurable indeed, in His greatness, yet whose attributes in some degree man is capable of cognising.

VI. Sufficiency of Natural Revelation.

The natural revelation of God is therefore not to be denied. A more vital question arises when we come to speak, next, of the *sufficiency* of this natural revelation. If man's developing mind, working on its natural environment, can reach so much truth about God, may it not fairly be argued, not only that this is all the knowledge of God which man *has*, but that it is all the knowledge he *needs*,—that it is sufficient for all the ends of his religious life? This question requires consideration.

1. One way which may be suggested of testing this point is to make the supposition—a quite unhistorical one, indeed,—of a mind which is a *perfectly pure mirror* of the natural revelation,—or, if one will, of a succession of such minds, with all the opportunities this gives for development,—minds capable of taking from the revelation the utmost it is able to yield,—and to ask: What, in such a case, would be the result? What would such a mind (or minds) be able to reach in the knowledge of God from its pure intuition, its sense of dependence, its impressions of nature, its observations of God's providence? Let the utmost be assumed. Let it be supposed that it is able to rise by assured steps to the thought of a great Author of the universe,—a God all-powerful,

all-wise, beneficent,—that in the strength of a firm moral conviction it grasps the truth of a providence ruling the world for moral ends,—that it is penetrated with reverence in presence of this Power, and is moved to the simpler acts of prayer and worship, —that in the events of life it thinks it can discern the guidance of God and answers to its prayers. Let it be assumed that, from other principles, in conjunction with the religious impulse, it attains the belief in the soul's survival of death, and in an enlarged and happier life hereafter.

2. It is perhaps not quite just to speak of this development of ideas as *merely* conjecture. There is, let it be owned, actually seen an approximation to what is here described, not only as a dim background in most historical religions, but in the beliefs held by the nobler minds of all ages—*e.g.*, by a Socrates, a Cleanthes, a Seneca, a Marcus Aurelius. And the question recurs—If natural revelation can yield thus much, is it not sufficient ? Is not this, after all, the real substance of religion ? When prophets and other good men received what they thought to be special revelations from God, may we not suspect that it was simply, in reality, this natural revelation of God which, in one or other of its forms, was making itself felt in their spirits ? In any case, when we strip off historical accidents, and seek 'the eternal truth' of religion, is it not to something like this we come back ? Are we not here, in short, in presence of the 'constants' of religion, of those parts of it which, in separation from 'dogmas' and doubtful historical facts, man's rational and moral consciousness can verify—in presence, therefore, of its *essential* parts ?

So unquestionably many in these days think. A little reflection, however, may modify this first impression, and produce the conviction of the urgent need of special and authoritative revelation for man's highest wants.

CHAPTER III

NEED OF SPECIAL REVELATION—BIBLICAL AND ETHNIC REVELATION

THE attempt has been made in the preceding chapter to do justice to the reality and scope of natural revelation. Some considerations may now be adduced to show that, grand and varied as nature's testimony to God is acknowledged to be, natural revelation alone is not adequate for the spiritual needs of mankind.

I. LIMITS OF NATURAL REVELATION.

1. A first thing to be observed is that, as was stated at the outset, the description given of *a perfectly pure mind*—a mind serving as the undimmed mirror of the natural revelation—is *entirely unhistorical.* A general sense or impression of the divine all ages and races of men have indeed manifested; individual thinkers have often risen to wonderfully clear and elevated views of God's being, character, and government; a confidence in an all-superintending providence, a rational rule of the world—in itself a kind of theism—may be traced in the nobler types of men in all periods of history. It is a fact just as certain, that no race or age has ever shown itself capable, by its own efforts, of rising to the height of the idea of God as just sketched, of grasping it clearly and steadily, and of connecting with it a pure

and spiritual worship. Impartial study shows the history of religion to have been rather that of the obscuration of what purer light may originally have been possessed; the sinking of mankind, as Paul depicts in Rom. i. 18 ff., into ever grosser polytheism and immorality.

It is, in short, one thing to admit that nature, in its objective aspect, reveals 'the everlasting power and divinity' of its Creator; and another to affirm that man, as modern theory regards him, with his untutored intellect, germinal conscience, undeveloped powers of reflection, and strong propensities to the sensuous and material, could evolve from that revelation all it was fitted to yield him, and create for himself a spiritual conception of God, and of his duty, such as is found in Holy Scripture. The pure mind which the hypothesis postulates is not there. It never was; and the picture which history yields of man in his religious development is not such as to yield high expectations of his achievements in the knowledge of God. Once man had lost the true idea of the divine, and permitted himself to become involved in the labyrinthine errors of polytheism, all evidence is against the idea of his ever being able to work himself out again.

From this first point of view, therefore, the light of nature would seem to be demonstrably insufficient for man's need. Something further,—a pure point of knowledge of God, the product of personal revelation,—must be given, if mankind is to attain such a knowledge of God as will furnish the ground of a pure, spiritual, and intelligent worship of Him; if it is to be saved from losing its way in an aberration becoming continuously the more hopeless. This original point of knowledge must be tended and developed by further revelations. The light vouchsafed must, for its preservation and enlargement, go on shining, in a succession of elect spirits, more and more unto the perfect day.

2. There is, however, a second and yet stronger call for special revelation. On the assumption yet made, the end of revelation would be reached if it furnished to man clearness and certainty on those truths embraced in the compass of natural revelation—*rational* and *necessary* truths. This was the view of revelation advocated by Lessing in his *Education of the Human Race*. Revelation was held to be necessary solely for the purpose of giving to man clearer knowledge and firmer assurance of truths which reason could either discover, or at least could be depended on ultimately to verify, for itself. Revelation is *illumination*. Its content is 'eternal truths,' and its end is to provide guidance for man till reason should be able to stand on its own feet.[1] The truth illumined does not go beyond the truth of reason and conscience, or that disclosed in nature and providence.

3. Ewald has drawn attention to one defect of any revelation which confines itself within these natural limits[2]—it is *general* and *indiscriminative*. Nature is a grand objective manifestation of the power and divinity of the Creator. But that power and divinity stand in no specific relation to the individual. It is a *general* revelation, like the overarching sky, often taken as its symbol, or like the sunshine, in which each has his share, but none a distinct property.

[1] Cf. on Lessing, Bruce, *The Chief End of Revelation*, pp. 17 ff.
[2] *Op. cit.* pp. 18 ff.

It is the same with reason and conscience, and with the sense of dependence. These yield, indeed, 'eternal truths' about God—ideas of Him as Rational Spirit, Author and Upholder of Moral law, the Absolute Power on which man and the universe depend. But the truth revealed is wholly general.

Now it should hardly need proof that religion, in the true idea of it, can never be satisfied with this general, almost impersonal relation to a God manifested in purely *universal* relations. Religion is in its essence a relation to a Being who stands, or is believed to stand, in a personal relation to His worshippers—a relation which can be satisfied only in personal communion. This is seen even on the ground of heathenism, a subject to which further reference will immediately be made. Heathenism is a constant attempt to find means of putting the worshipper and his god into personal relations with each other. This is much more manifest in the Biblical religion, in which the craving of the soul is ever for immediate, conscious, personal relation to God; for the personal assurance that God is gracious to it. This is the nerve of the piety of the psalms, and of all true religion. 'As the hart panteth after the water-brooks, so panteth my soul after Thee, O God.'[1] All this, however, it should be obvious, is possible only on the basis of a relation more determinate than that yielded by the general revelation of God in nature. It means that God has descended from the sphere of *general* unto that of *special* revelation; that He has come to man in some form of self-manifestation, and given him His

[1] Ps. xlii. 1.

sure word, on which He has caused him to hope.[1] Supposing man to have attained to the most perfect ideas of God conceivable through natural revelation, this still would not satisfy the inmost craving of religion, which is, not simply that man should know *about* God, but that he should get into living, personal, relations of friendship *with* Him.

4. This is to regard the need of revelation from the side of *man*. But the need and presumption of special revelation may be shown to follow with equal stringency from *the right idea of God*. Man's heart is yearning for a word of God, a sign or token of recognition and love. Is God, on His side, to remain everlastingly silent ? Assume the theistic, which is likewise the Christian, position, that God is a personal, self-conscious, ethical, self-revealing Being,—a Being whose nature is Fatherly love, who made man in His own image, and seeks to draw him into fellowship with Himself,—a Being who desires to make Himself known to man, and to be known, loved, and served by man,—is it conceivable that He should remain for ever behind the veil of nature, and be content to sustain to man only the impersonal, indefinite relation already described ? In man there is implanted the impulse to seek after God. Is there no corresponding impulse in God to draw near to man, and unveil Himself to him ? To quote Ewald again : 'How then should He not answer the earnestly perseveringly questioning spirit of man,— He of whose Spirit man's is but a human reflection and an enkindled spark, and to whom in his searching and questioning He can draw near quite otherwise than to the visible things in creation ?'[2] The

[1] Ps. cxix. 49. [2] *Op. cit.* p. 18.

striving, seeking, attaining—is it to be all on man's side? Is it enough to say: 'God is *there*; let man find Him out'?

It is not a sufficient reply to urge that God does not thus stand aloof; that He is already there in this very striving, stimulating the soul into search after Himself. He is behind the veil all the while, aiding man's efforts, quickening his aspirations, secretly answering his prayers. For, on the theory, God does *not* draw near to meet the soul whose striving He has secretly incited. And why only in secret? Why invisible and silent, when He has the power to speak, to reassure, to help? It is not enough, again, to use the word 'love.' For an inactive love,—a love that does not display itself in words or deeds,—can satisfy no one. A general benevolence cannot take the place of love. If God is truly love, He may be expected to manifest His love in seeking closer, personal, relations with man. It follows, as has been argued elsewhere,[1] that the only Theism which can remain tenable is a Theism which completes itself in a doctrine of special revelation. The word 'law'—to some almost a fetish—need terrify no one in this connection. Without anticipating later discussion, the one thing that may be held certain *a priori* of the Almighty Author of the universe, assuming Him to be personal, free, and loving, is that He will not bind His hands by natural ordinances in any such way as will preclude His effective interposition for the help of His moral creatures, when they need and seek His help.

5. To adduce only one other consideration on

[1] Cf. *The Christian View of God and the World*, pp. 62-5.

this subject—if the need of revelation follows from a true idea of God, and of religion as personal fellowship, it as surely follows from a right idea of the *plan of the world.* History is not, any more than nature, given up to fortuity. God has His plan and end in it, the supreme end, as Kant rightly deduced, being the establishment of a perfect moral fellowship, or Kingdom of God, among men. Such a plan is not wrought out automatically, or through impersonal, unconsciously working laws of evolution. It can only be wrought out along definite lines, through the conscious, intelligent, voluntary, co-operation of men. But how is man ever to co-operate intelligently with God in the furtherance of His world-purpose if he is left wholly in the dark about it? How can he ever be trusted to discover it for himself, or to know the part God wills him to take in it? Is it a higher view of history, to regard man as groping and stumbling in the dark, or to conceive of him as taken in hand by God, taught and disciplined by God, in a manner suitable to each stage in the development of His purpose, made an intelligent co-worker with God in the accomplishment of His ends? If this plan of God is further regarded, as in Christianity, as redemptive and remedial—a work of grace from its inception to its consummation—the need of revelation to enable man to avail himself of its provision, and to realise its aims, is seen to be imperative.

II. Heathen Need of Revelation.

The considerations now advanced suffice, it is hoped, to show the need and the reasonableness of special revelation, as well as to create a powerful presumption in its favour. There is good sense in a remark of Paley's, in the commencement of his *Evidences*, which may be here quoted. 'I deem it unnecessary,' he says, 'to prove that mankind stood in need of a revelation, because I have met with no serious person who thinks that, even under the Christian revelation, we have too much light or any degree of assurance which is superfluous.' He adds: 'I desire moreover that, in judging of Christianity, it may be remembered, that the question lies between this religion and none; for, if the Christian religion be not credible, no one, with whom we have to do, will support the pretension of any other.'

If confirmation of this need of special revelation be required, it can be found in abundance on the field of *Heathenism*. Not infrequently, by way of discrediting the Biblical claim to revelation, appeal is made to the widespread craving for revelation, and the attempts to satisfy this craving, in the heathen world. The oracles, divinations, necromancies, and other modes of interrogating the unseen, are dwelt upon, and it is asked—Does not this evidence of a universal belief in revelation, and eagerness in seeking after it, prove that the claim to special revelation in the Bible must be dismissed as baseless?

In reality the phenomena in question prove the very opposite. The craving for communion with the unseen manifested in them [1] may not prove that

[1] Cf. Pfleiderer, *Phil. of Rel.* iv. pp. 48-9. The juggler and the charlatan, he says, traded 'on the need of revelation felt alike by people and by sages.'

the oracles, auguries, soothsayings, and like superstitions in heathen religions are true; but they do prove the profound and inextinguishable need which has ever been felt in heathenism for special revelation. The one thing they show to demonstration is, that, whoever is satisfied with the measure of knowledge of God given in natural revelation, it is not the people who are left to that revelation, or whose light is dimmer than our own. In all ages these have eagerly desired more, and, in default of such better revelation, have sought to still their craving by resort to oracles and sorceries.[1] It is not the lower order of minds only that have experienced this craving. It is the *sages* of heathenism who have felt the need most profoundly. The brilliant philosophical systems of the ancient world gave neither certainty nor content; in Greece and Rome alike they are seen ending in scepticism. A universal uncertainty on the highest questions of existence was the most marked feature of the age in which Christ appeared. As Plato affirmed, the Father of all is hard to find, and, when He is found, it is impossible to make Him known to all.[2] And in the *Phaedo* he makes the friend of Socrates express

[1] Cf. Orelli, *Prophecy* (E. T.), p. 23: 'The universal search of the nations for revelation of the Deity and indications of His will proves a vividly-felt need of self-revelation on His part, a need making itself directly felt in man as he stands with childlike simplicity in presence of God and nature. But, although points of attachment were given to the nations in nature and history, intellect, and conscience, in which they might discern the Deity, still the uncertain superstitious, inquisitive, and insane feeling after a divine revelation beyond the sphere in which God was pleased to make Himself known to them, show how little these revelations could satisfy the natural man, with his nature corrupted and his power of perception weakened by sin.'

[2] In the *Timaeus*.

the need for some word of God which will more surely and safely carry them when the raft of human opinion fails.[1]

III. Biblical and Ethnic Revelation.

Suppose now, however, it is granted that special revelation, as alone adequate to satisfy the religious needs, and support true faith in God and His purpose, is not only possible and reasonable, but is probable, the question of the relation of heathenism to revelation is by no means exhausted. The probability of special, supernatural revelation—supernatural in the sense of transcending, not in that of contradicting, the natural—may justify us in looking for such a revelation along the path of the history of Israel, and supremely in Christ; but the question remains to be asked: Is this privilege *confined* to Israel? If, as is affirmed, natural revelation is insufficient for man's higher needs, and heathenism itself craves for something better, is it to be supposed that all the nations except Israel have been left through the long millenniums of their history with only the light of natural

[1] 'For I dare say,' says Simias, 'that you, Socrates, feel as I do, how very hard or almost impossible is the attainment of any certainty about questions such as these in the present life, and yet I should deem him a coward who did not prove what is said about them to the uttermost, or whose heart failed him before he had examined them on every side. For he should persevere, until he has attained one of two things: either he should discover or learn the truth about them; or, if this is impossible, I would have him take the best and most irrefragable of human notions, and let this be the raft upon which he sails through life—not without risk, as I admit, if he cannot find some sure word of God which will more surely and safely carry him' (*Phaedo*, sect. 85, Jowett's trans.).

revelation—that special revelation has been wholly denied to them?

In answering this question, extremes meet. On the one hand are found those who would deny to the nations—to the whole Gentile world—special revelation in any form or degree. God has left them, it is thought, to their own unaided faculties, in the use of the light of nature, in seeking after Him. No supernatural assistance has been vouchsafed. On the other hand, as already seen, are those—the majority in our own day—who break down the distinction of natural and supernatural altogether. This class will admit no distinction in origin between Gentile religions and Israel's. They see revelation as truly in the one as in the other. As this commonly is found to mean that there is no true supernatural revelation in either case, the two views come, at bottom, as regards heathenism, much to the same thing.

1. In dealing with this question, a first thing to be pointed out is that, whatever place is allowed to special revelation in heathenism, it cannot affect the broad fact, historically attested, that heathen religions were *without the light of a clear, authoritative, supernatural revelation*, such as Israel, alone of all nations, possessed. It is the contrast so clearly discernible between the religion of Israel and other religions in this respect which compels the impartial investigator to assign to the former a special origin. This also is the broad teaching of the Scripture on God's dealing with the nations. The nations are described as 'suffered' for the time 'to walk in their own ways.'[1] They are described as in ignorance of

[1] Acts xiv. 16.

the true God and of the way of life.[1] 'The times of this ignorance,' Paul says, 'God overlooked; but now He commandeth men that they should all everywhere repent.'[2] With this corresponds the peculiar consciousness which Israel at all times had of its exceptional position as a people standing in special relation to God. 'For what great nation is there, that hath a god so nigh unto them, as the Lord our God is whensoever we call upon him? . . . For ask now of the days that are past, which were before thee, since the day that God created man upon the earth, and from the one end of heaven unto the other, whether there hath been any such thing as this great thing is, or hath been heard like it?'[3] If Israel was a vine trained and planted by the hand of God,[4] heathenism can be regarded at best as a vine growing wild.

2. While this is so, it is next to be remarked that a special revelation in Israel is not incompatible with the view that *in many special ways* God was present also in heathenism, imparting to heathen peoples measures of His light and grace. The nations of men were never, at any period of their history, left wholly without revelation. Apart from what may be said of a 'primitive revelation' the light of which was never wholly lost,[5] this is evidenced in many ways. Paul, in the discourse at Athens above quoted, defines the end of God's dealings with the nations: 'That they should seek God, if haply they might feel after Him and find Him,' but does not fail to add: 'Though He is not far from each

[1] Acts xvii. 23; Eph. ii. 12; iv. 18.
[2] Acts xvii. 30.
[3] Deut. iv. 7, 32-35.
[4] Ps. lxxx. 8-10; Is. v. 1-7.
[5] See below, p. 64.

one of us.'[1] Elsewhere he says: 'Yet He left not Himself without witness';[2] and though the reference is mainly to the natural revelation of God's goodness (giving them rains and fruitful seasons), it need not be supposed that the revelation was confined to this. The Scripture gives numerous indications to the contrary. In Abraham's time is found Melchizedek, a 'priest of God Most High'—a man evidently of high and enlightened ideas—at Salem.[3] In Moses' time is the strange figure of Balaam, a prophet of Jehovah, outside Israel, at Pethor, by the Euphrates.[4] Numerous instances occur of revelations and warnings to heathen kings in dreams (Abimelech, Pharaoh, Nebuchadnezzar, etc.),[5] and by prophets (Jonah: the prophetic oracles to the nations). Job and his friends in the land of Uz are represented as not without the light of revelation.[6] Cyrus is announced as raised up and girded by God for the work he had to do.[7] If, as Peter affirmed, 'in every nation he that feareth [God], and worketh righteousness, is acceptable to Him,'[8] is it to be believed that God does not draw near to such seekers with His light, His succours, His answers to prayer? Or may we not look to heathenism itself? It is a Christian doctrine that the sages and teachers of heathen peoples received from God's special illumination whatever measure of the light of truth they professed. The light of the Logos, 'which lighteth every man,'[9] as the early Fathers taught,[10] shone in them. 'If we

[1] Acts xvii. 27. [2] Acts xiv. 17. [3] Gen. xiv. 18-20.
[4] Num. xxii. 5 ff. [5] Gen. xx. 3, 6; xli.; Dan. ii., etc.
[6] Job iv. 12 ff.; xxxviii. ff.; xlii. [7] Is. xlv. 1 ff.
[8] Acts x. 35. [9] John i. 9.
[10] The doctrine of the 'spermatic' Logos—the Logos as implanting

reflect,' writes John Calvin, 'that the Spirit of God is the only fountain of truth, we will be careful, as we would avoid offering insult to Him, not to reject or contemn truth wherever it appears. In despising the gifts, we insult the Giver. How, then, can we deny that truth must have beamed in those ancient law-givers who arranged civil order and discipline with so much equity? . . . Nay, we cannot read the writings of the ancients on these subjects without the highest admiration: an admiration which their excellence will not allow us to withhold. But shall we deem anything to be noble and praiseworthy, without tracing it to the hand of God?'[1] In brief, at no time has God withdrawn His interest, care, providential guidance, help, revelation, from any heathen people.

3. Without professing to penetrate into what must always remain more or less a mystery—the ways of God in His dealings with heathen peoples—it is perhaps possible to see in general *wherein the broad contrast existed*, in respect of revelation, between them and the people of Israel. It is not simply that revelation in Israel had a fulness, clearness, and certainty, a strong and authoritative note, which it lacked in heathenism; though that also is true. The deeper cause lay in the *content* of the revelation, and in its connection with a developing redemptive purpose, working onwards, in continuous historical process, to a definite goal. Revelation in heathenism, so far as that is to be recognised, was of a more partial, sporadic, individual character;

the seeds of truth in heathen minds—is prominent in Justin Martyr (1 Apol. 46; 2 Apol. 8-13), Clement, Origen, etc.

[1] *Institutes*, bk. II. ch. ii. 15, 16; cf. bk. III. ch. xiv. 2, etc.

it lacked the creative, continuous, progressive character which it had in the chosen race. There is a great difference, manifestly, between revelations which are purely personal and private, and revelations, like those to Abraham and Moses, which enter into a history of the Kingdom of God, and form part of a series, extending through ages, and conducting to an end of world-wide significance. In no case do we find revelation outside Israel assuming the marked, unmistakable, historical, and visibly supernatural form it took in that nation. In character it consisted more in *illumination*—an illumination on the basis of the natural revelation, making that clearer, deepening receptivity for it, interpreting its lessons through experience. In Israel revelation had a character of universality; an aspect to the world; it brought in truths, and founded relations, which held in them the promise of a future. It is mainly this positive historical character which distinguishes it from revelation to the nations outside.[1]

IV. LIMITATION OF HISTORICAL REVELATION.

If the question be still pressed, Why should revelation have taken this form of limitation it did?—why should other peoples not have been favoured

[1] Dorner remarks: 'Divine activity, if it is to be called revelation, must impart something analogous to the product of creation, something new, not previously existent in the spirit. . . . Revelation denotes not merely the introduction of something new to the individual, but its introduction by God's action to the race as a whole for the first time. . . . Mere capacity for religion is an insignificant matter in comparison with that which will be the issue of historical facts, or God's acts of institution' (*Op. cit.* ii. pp. 134-9).

with as full and gracious a revelation as Israel had?—it is to be admitted that the answer is one which lies largely beyond us in the depths of God's own unsearchable wisdom and counsel.[1] Any partial answer that can be given must be sought for in the *ends* which God had in view alike in His giving and His withholding.[2] Here such considerations as the following occur:—

1. It is necessary to remember, as one element in the case, the *responsibility of the nations* in parting with the light they originally had. From the Biblical point of view, however it may be in the view of evolutionary science, the nations were not guiltless in this respect. 'That which may be known of God is manifest in them; for God manifested it unto them . . . that they may be without excuse; because that, knowing God, they glorified Him not as God, neither gave thanks, but became vain in their reasonings, and their senseless heart was darkened.'[3] A responsibility, therefore, rested on mankind for the state of ignorance, error, and moral corruption into which it had come. It follows that special revelation, in every instance in which it was granted, was an act of grace. In historical revelation the calling of Abraham, the early promises, the raising up of Moses, the covenant with Israel, the sending of prophets, were due wholly to grace.

2. It is further to be considered, assuming the need of historical revelation, that it was only by the *choice of a particular individual*, afterwards of

[1] Cf. Rom. xi. 33.

[2] Butler's *Analogy*, pt. II. ch. vi., on 'The Want of Universality in Revelation,' may be compared.

[3] Rom. i. 19, 21. Cf. Dorner, *Op. cit.* ii. pp. 245-8.

a nation, that God *could* work out His gracious purpose for the blessing of mankind. Historical revelation had to begin *somewhere*, in the choice of a special person, the preparing of a special people, the providing for 'an election of grace' within this people, in order that the world might ultimately be universally enlightened and benefited. Israel was to be God's messenger to the world—a 'light of the Gentiles.'[1] A definite line of historical development had to be adopted if the desired end was to be reached. This is the law of election in the divine economy. Election is not arbitrary. It is not an act of personal favouritism, but always, as in the case of Abraham, a means to a larger blessing.[2]

3. The subject is looked at yet more comprehensively when it is recalled that the heathen peoples had *their own mission*, and that their mission was not that of the people of Israel. It is not to deny a divine providence in heathenism to say that the *charismata* bestowed on heathen peoples were other than religious. In heathenism it is the secular consciousness that predominates. To it is given the development of civilisation,—of arts, laws, letters, philosophy, states,—of productivity on the *worldly* side. In Israel the religious vocation is the central one. The sages even of heathenism grasped truth from the civil, political, philosophical sides, rather than from the religious. A prophet of Israel, therefore, would not have found receptivity among the heathen, even had he risen among them. The soil was not there on which the seed of divine truth could be sown, or from which it might be propagated. To secure this a people had to be prepared.

[1] Is. xlii. 6; lx. 1-3. [2] Gen. xii. 1-3.

There had to be concentration to gain the ποῦ στῶ necessary to act upon the world. A community of grace had to be built up from the very commencement. Hence, again, the significance of such a fact as the Call of Abraham ; the meaning of the hedging round and training of the people of Israel, till sufficient force was accumulated for larger, wider action.

4. Lastly, may it not truthfully be said that it was as essential to the divine purpose that heathenism should be left for the time *freely to develop itself*, as that Israel should be placed under special divine training for the purposes of its mission ? It was not left, certainly, to develop unguided or unrestrained. But it was left to develop *freely*, even in respect of the God-denying tendency it had taken into its heart, that this might be revealed, and its real character become manifest. Civilisation, arts, philosophy, science, were permitted to do their utmost, not only for the sake of their positive gains to humanity, but that the moral helplessness of a world without God might be set in its strongest light. This is no arbitrary procedure on the part of God. It rests on the eternal law that under the government of God everything that is, even evil, must be permitted to manifest its full nature. 'For nothing,' Jesus said, 'is hid, that shall not be made manifest ; nor anything secret, that shall not be known and come to light.'[1] Only as evil, once it has entered, is permitted to reveal its whole nature, can it be effectually overcome. How otherwise can God's patience, in permitting evil to rise to the heights it often does, be explained ?

[1] Luke viii. 17.

V. Question of a Primitive Revelation.

A question germane to the present discussion may here receive a little further attention, viz., the value to be attached to the idea of a 'primitive revelation.' Such an idea seems to many investigators of the philosophy of religion no longer worthy of consideration. Dr. G. T. Ladd, *e.g.*, in his recent large and able work on *The Philosophy of Religion*, directs much reasoning against the notions of 'a primitive revelation' and 'a primitive monotheism.'[1] As opposed to these notions, the words of Zeller are endorsed as 'undoubtedly correct': 'What humanity possesses of religious truth and religious life it must win for itself. . . . Religion, like any human work, could only climb upward gradually, out of crude and imperfect beginnings, to a nobler and more pure form.'[2] Is not such a *dictum*, however, itself as *a priori* as anything on the other side can be? Is it not, besides, in contradiction with facts, which show, in many cases, 'undoubtedly' a descent in religion from relatively simpler and purer to grosser and growingly polytheistic forms?

1. On the question of a 'primitive revelation' it is permissible to think that there is a certain confusion of idea. No one seriously contends, as Dr. Ladd and others apparently suppose, that religion 'originated'[3] in a primitive divine revelation. Such an idea is on the face of it untenable. But it is not untenable to suppose that man had, from the first, *together with* his inherent religious endowment, a measure of divine revelation granted

[1] *Op. cit.* pp. 152, 204, 223, etc. [2] P. 151. [3] P. 152.

to him sufficient at least to ground, in an elementary way, a pure worship of God, and keep him right in his relations with God. The fact of such revelation may be, as Dr. Ladd says, beyond the conditions of 'historical,' *i.e.*, extra-Scriptural proof, but there is no warrant in history or anything else for denying either its possibility or its probability.[1] If revelation is conceded at all, it is difficult to see why it should not begin early as well as late. It is not, surely, to serious reflection, a higher idea of God to suppose that He should have left man to grow up from a semi-brutish, or at least rude and barbarian state, deeply entangled in sin, error, and idolatry, before giving him some clear knowledge of Himself, and of the way of worshipping Him, than to suppose that He should have put Himself, as the Bible says He did, into moral relations with His creature at the first, giving him some assured light for his guidance.

2. As respects 'primitive monotheism,' this also is an ambiguous phrase, for it is not supposed by any that man set out with an abstract conception of the unity of God in formal opposition to the idea of false gods or of many gods. Enough for the soul

[1] Dr. Ladd is well aware of the nests of fallacies which lurk in current speculations about 'primitive man,' and some of the most valuable portions of his work are those which deal with this subject. 'Strictly speaking,' he says, 'little or nothing is known of primitive man' (p. 14). 'One must not be imposed on by an offhand transference of the characteristics of savages or uncivilised tribes as now existing to the case of primitive man. To quote from the highest authority in anthropology (Waitz), the "primitive man" is a pure fiction, however convenient a fiction he may be' (p. 135). He trenchantly criticises the tendency to set up fetishism, totemism, ancestor-worship, or the like, as the 'primitive form' of religion (pp. 96-9, 106, 142 ff., 148, 170, etc.).

to realise that it was in the presence of its Maker, and of the Lord of All. On philosophical and historical grounds it is quite as reasonable to believe that at the root of the religious consciousness there lay a yet undifferentiated sense of the divine—a sense afterwards refracted or broken up into the polytheism we know of—as that monotheism was a late development from a low-grade fetishism or spirit-worship, or the imaginative spiritualising of natural objects.

The interest of this question in the present connection is that, in the Biblical conception, in marked contrast with 'modern' tendencies, there is no period in the history of the world when man was without some degree of special revelation. God is assumed to have had dealings with man—to have spoken with man—in the very dawn of his history; and the piety of the godly in the primitive age, as in the ages that came after, had revelation as its basis. The piety, indeed, is of the simplest and most unrestrained kind, hardly going beyond the bounds of natural revelation. But it is non-idolatrous, non-mythological, spiritual, and is represented, in its clearness, certainty, and assurance of acceptance, as the product of 'faith.'[1] One is impressed here with the *reserve* of the Biblical notices, so unlike what one finds in heathenism, but not less with the fact of revelation they imply. 'Then began men to call on the name of the Lord.'[2] 'Enoch walked with God.'[3] This primitive piety holds in it already the germ of 'promise'[4] of which the long history of subsequent revelation is the unfolding.

[1] Cf. Heb. xi. 4 ff.
[2] Gen. iv. 26.
[3] Gen. v. 24.
[4] Gen. iii. 15.

CHAPTER IV

REVELATION AND HISTORY—FORMS OF SPECIAL REVELATION

It was before mentioned as one of the chief gains in the modern treatment of revelation that attention is increasingly concentrated on revelation as something distinctively *historical*. In all cases, indeed, the divine *act* is connected with the divine *word*, without which its meaning would not be intelligible. With the *external* or objective element in revelation there is everywhere connected an *internal*. But the historical element in the Biblical revelation is still that which gives it its distinctive character. Without this it would be, in great part, in the air. In proportion as confidence in the history is shaken, the foundation of the whole structure of revelation is weakened.

I. Historical Revelation in the Old Testament.

A question of much importance for the doctrine of revelation thus arises as to *the value* of the historical element in the Biblical religion. The facts of revelation in the New Testament will be dealt with later; at present attention may be directed to the history in the Old Testament, and to the degree in which that is affected by recent critical discussion.[1]

1. The Old Testament assumes the reality of *a historical revelation* of God from man's creation till the close of the prophetic age. It is, on its own showing, the record of this revelation. A continuous thread of history unites its end with its beginning, One thing manifest in the survey of this history is that, while the parts are *organically* related, yet the history does not flow on evenly or uniformly, but falls into periods of epoch-making importance—*creative* periods, as they may be named,—and periods which, relatively to the former, are not creative, but what may be called *continuative*; [2]—periods when the forces of revelation are acting, as it were, at their maximum (*e.g.*, the Call of Abraham, the Exodus and Law-giving), and periods in which the spirit of revelation is still, indeed, active, but chiefly on the basis of what has been already revealed, and as preparatory to a new advance. A few words must suffice to indicate the chief stages.

The earliest period in the history of God's dealing with man—the *primitive* and *antediluvian*—has already been referred to. It covers what is told of Paradise, the Fall, the lines of Seth and Cain, the Flood. In it, in a sense, is laid the foundation of all else in the Bible.

The period next succeeding is that *from Noah*, with whom is connected a definite epoch through

[1] The author can, naturally, only speak as he believes, and the lines he follows are those already laid down in his special work on the subject (*Problem of the O. T.*). Criticism, in his view, has become side-tracked, and is bound, ere long, to retrace many of its steps.

[2] Dorner aptly compares the original and continuative forms of revelation to the relation of creation and conservation.

the covenant made with him,[1] *to Abraham.* In this period mankind again multiplies, and is distributed in its families and nations throughout the earth.[2] This, according to the Bible, takes place in connection with the judgment at Babel.[3] The divine providence fixes the bounds of the nations.[4] The period is marked by the growing obscuration of the consciousness of God—that confusion of God and the world which is the root error of heathenism,[5] and the loss of the sense of the unity of God in polytheism.[6] Hence the need of a new beginning in special revelation, in the call of, and covenant with, Abraham.

The history now moves on through the covenants, promises, and providential dealings of God with the chosen family in the *patriarchal* age. Then follows, in fulfilment of these promises, the *Mosaic* age, with the Exodus, the Sinaitic Covenant and Law-giving, the wilderness discipline, till the settlement in Canaan. After an interval of disorganisation under the Judges, a new period begins with the *monarchy*, and the fresh nucleus of promises connected with the house of David.[7] The unhappy division of the kingdom, and the separate histories and backslidings of Israel and Judah, lead up to the age of *prophecy*—though in the wider sense there

[1] Gen. ix.

[2] Gen. x. The value of the Table of Nations in Gen. x. has been greatly enhanced by recent discovery. Professor Kautzsch says: 'The so-called table of nations remains, according to all results of monumental exploration, an ethnographic, original monument of the first rank, which nothing can replace' (*Die Bleibende Bedeutung des A. T.*, p. 17).

[3] On this, see Schelling's suggestive remarks, quoted by Auberlen, *Div. Rev.*, pp. 160-2.

[4] Deut. xxxii. 8; Acts, xvii. 26.

[5] Cf. Dorner, as above.

[6] Josh. xxiv. 2.

[7] 2 Sam. vii.

were prophets from the beginning.[1] A great crisis in this period is connected with the notable figures of Elijah and Elisha, when the choice in the Northern kingdom had come to be between Jehovah and Baal. The very disappointments and chastisements of the prophetic age[2]—the fall of the Northern kingdom, Assyrian and Chaldean invasions, etc.—had priceless results in aiding the disengaging of the idea of the Kingdom of God from its existing political form, in distinguishing the true kernel of Israel ('the remnant') from Israel after the flesh, in evoking visions, promises, and hopes of a better economy, and in giving further and more definite shape to the idea of the Messiah. The *Exile* ended the kingdom of Judah, and prepared the way, after the return, for the new theocracy, when, purged from idolatry, the nation, in renewed covenant with God, applied itself with settled aim to the keeping of *the law of Moses.* In one sense this was a backward step, for life dominated by the law fell far short of the glowing spiritual ideals of the prophets, and tended to the legalism into which the nation afterwards sank; but it was for that time the only form of organisation suited to the people, and might have yielded better fruit than it did, had the spirit of the people been more upright, and

[1] Gen. xx. 7; Num. xi. 27; Deut. xxxiv. 10; Hos. xii. 13; Acts iii. 18, 21, etc.

[2] W. R. Smith has said: 'The work of the prophets of the Assyrian and Babylonian periods falls in the most critical stage of the history of the religion of Israel—when, humanly speaking, it seemed far from improbable that that religion would sink to the level of common Semitic heathenism, and perish like the religions of the Semitic peoples, with the political fall of the nation that professed it' (*The Prophets*, p. 18).

the lessons of the prophets, whose memories were at length honoured, been more laid to heart.

2. Such, in bare outline, is the picture which the Bible presents of the course of the history of revelation in Israel. This picture, it is well known, undergoes entire *transformation* at the hands of *modern critical scholarship*. The real course of events, it is held by many modern scholars, is nearly the precise reverse of that just described. The law, in the new scheme, comes in at the end, instead of at the beginning of Israel's history, and the history itself is recast from its first page to its last. The actual process in the history of the religion, it is declared, was one of gradual development from small and poor beginnings; the patriarchs are legendary or ideal figures, representing perhaps early tribal movements; Moses, if such a person ever existed, is largely a legendary creation; the history of the Exodus in any case is mostly legendary. So with the Conquest, and in no small measure with the history of the Judges and of the earlier kings.

It need not occasion surprise if this 'critical' view of Israel's history is felt by many, by no means narrow-minded, to be well-nigh fatal to the pretensions of the Old Testament to be a record of a real divine revelation. It must at least be owned that, if a supernatural revelation has been given, the real history of it, on this reading of the facts, has been displaced by another mainly legendary and fictitious. It is not on such a basis that the present writer can undertake to defend the reality of revelation and inspiration in the Old Testament. Nor, convinced as he is that, despite its present vogue among scholars, the evolutionary, critical theory of the religion of Israel is not the true one, and that in criticism itself, in archæology, in a better knowledge of the ancient world, in a deeper understanding of the ideas of the religion of Israel, forces are surely working to make this evident, does he feel that he is called to undertake such a task. The reasons for his non-acceptance of the current critical scheme he has given elsewhere, and need not here repeat. But a few results, in their bearing on the subject in hand, may be indicated.

The documentary analysis of the Pentateuch, and other results of purely literary criticism (doubtful as many of these are held to be), may be left untouched. They are secondary in importance to the leading question of the reliableness of the historical content. The general trustworthiness of the history, as has already been indicated, is, apart from other reasons, believed to be internally guaranteed by the depth and organic character—the forward movement under the direction of a divine purpose—of the ideas embodied in it. Here, on the surface of the record, is something which it lies beyond the capacity of irresponsible editors or collectors of legends, or even of late prophetically-minded men, to invent, or introduce into the substance of a national folk-lore. The religion which unfolds itself in the history of the Old Testament is *one* religion, moving on with stately, serious step—grave, monotheistic, progressive. It is unfolded with a divine coherence, and ever-increasing breadth of scope, depth of meaning, and prophetic insight into the future. It has, as Dorner says of it,[1] teleology as

[1] *Op. cit.* i. p. 274.

its soul. God is in it, in the displays of His holiness, majesty, faithfulness, and grace. The purpose it embodies does not halt till it rests in Christ.

For any one taking this view of the Old Testament history, it will be found difficult to believe that the patriarchs are the wholly mythical or legendary figures many would make them out to be, or that the covenants and promises of that early age are unreal. It will be found difficult to believe that Moses was not divinely raised up and commissioned, and did not, by divine command, lead the enslaved Israelites out of Egypt, and across the Red Sea, to form at Sinai a religious covenant between them and Jehovah, which pledged them ever after to be His people. It will be found difficult to believe that Moses did not then and after give to the people laws and ordinances—both civil and priestly—in substance identical with those in the books which record his legislation. It will be found difficult to believe that Deuteronomy is not, as it claims to be,[1] a reproduction of actual discourses which the law-giver, before his death, delivered in the plains of Moab, on the borders of the land of promise. It will be found difficult to believe that the Conquest was not effected by Joshua and the tribes in the general manner depicted in the Book of Joshua. And so with the remainder of the history.

All this can be maintained, without insisting on any overstrained theory of 'inerrancy' in historical detail, and while freely granting that much in the literary form and dramatic presentation of the narrative belongs to the *telling* of the story—the shape it had acquired in tradition, and is, there-

[1] Deut. xxxi. 9, 24.

fore, not to be unduly pressed. It is possible to concede this, and yet to be persuaded that the history, even in its early parts, rests, as becomes a history of revelation, on well-preserved tradition and sound historical knowledge, to which from a very early period—earlier, probably, than most are accustomed to think—documentary material contributed;—further, that this was not a work of man's mind merely, but one in which the Spirit of God was actively present, to the very end that such a faithful record of revelation might be provided. In support of such a view appeal may be made again to the internal character of the history; but also, now more than ever, to the confirmations and corroborations of some of the oldest and most contested statements in the sacred record. Such old documents, *e.g.*, as the Table of Nations in Gen. x., referred to above, and the account of Chedorlaomer's expedition in Gen. xiv., shine, in the light of modern exploration, in a new lustre of historical trustworthiness.[1]

II. Highest Types of Revelation—Moses and Christ.

The way is now open for considering more particularly the nature and forms of special revelation; but, before entering on details, it may serve a useful purpose to glance briefly at the highest and most perfect forms in which revelation is presented in the Bible—those, viz., in *Moses* and in *Christ*. It cannot

[1] Cf. in illustration of this part of the subject, *Problem of O. T.*, ch. xi., 'Archæology and the O. T.'; and *The Bible Under Trial*, ch. vi., 'Archæology as Searchlight.'

but be observed that revelation in the Old Testament and the New circles specially round these two poles. With Moses are connected the prophets;[1] with Christ the apostles.[2] There is, indeed, as has already been seen, an earlier stage—the patriarchal, likewise connected with an epoch-making name: Abraham's. But Moses and Christ remain the great, the outstanding, figures in revelation. 'The law was given through Moses; grace and truth came through Jesus Christ.'[3] And when we study these figures carefully, we perceive, notwithstanding the immeasurable distance that separates them—Moses, the servant in the house, and Christ, the Son over His own house[4]—a certain analogy in their positions.

To look first at Christ. Here the thing which must chiefly strike the attentive reader of the Gospels about Christ, regarded as Revealer, is His perfect unity of mind and will with God—what we may call, with Ritschl, His 'solidarity' with God. While recognising in Christ One who is filled with the Spirit beyond measure,[5] it does not readily occur to us, in reading the Gospel narratives, to think or speak of Christ as 'inspired.' The unity of mind of Christ and God is too intimate for that. It cannot but be noticed, further, that, while Christ is unceasing in His inculcation of the duty of 'faith' on others, He never in a single instance speaks of Himself as having 'faith' in God, or 'believing' in God. The reason is the obvious one that in Christ 'knowledge' in relation to God—pure, immediate, reciprocal, perfect knowledge—takes the place of what is 'faith' in us. 'No one knoweth the Son, save the

[1] Matt. vii. 12; Luke, xvi. 31; xxiv. 17, etc.
[2] Eph. ii. 20.
[3] John, i. 17.
[4] Heb. iii. 5, 6.
[5] John, iii. 34.

Father; neither doth any one know the Father, save the Son, and he to whom the Son willeth to reveal Him.'[1] Faith in us is the response to this revelation which Christ gives of the Father. But Christ had no other to act as the medium of revelation to Him. He drew directly from the divine source. The manner of this perfect intersphering of knowledge of Christ and the Father—an intersphering which gave to Christ at all points in His earthly life a knowledge of the purpose and will of the Father—is part of that 'mystery of godliness'[2] which we can never hope fully to penetrate. But the fact is *there*—not less evident in the Synoptics than in the Fourth Gospel; and it presents us with the perfect type of revelation.

Now it is worthy of observation that it is an *approach* to this higher mode of revelation—though necessarily on an immensely lower level—which is attributed to Moses, the founder of the old dispensation, as Christ is of the new. It is thus that the position of Moses is differentiated from that of succeeding prophets—that, while the Lord made Himself known to these in dark speeches, He knew Moses face to face, and spoke to him mouth to mouth.[3] There was an immediacy, freedom, and unveiled character in the intercourse of Moses with God which suited the place of honour he occupied, and the work he had to do, in the economy of revelation; and on this height of privilege he stood alone till *the* Prophet like unto Moses[4] appeared in

[1] Matt. xi. 27. [2] 1 Tim. iii. 16.

[3] Num. xii. 6-8; Deut. xxxiv. 10. Something of the same kind is suggested of Abraham—the earlier great figure in revelation—in Is. xli. 8: 'Abraham my friend.'

[4] Deut. xviii. 15; Acts, vii. 37.

the fulness of the times. There will seem to many a supreme improbability in the supposition that, holding this unique place in the history of revelation, Moses should be the dim and legendary figure which modern critical theories assert.

It is in any case to be remarked that the higher prophetic consciousness of a later age never attained to the altitude here assigned to Moses. Even where trance and vision are transcended, as generally they are in the higher prophecy, the prophet still struggles with his message as with something distinct from himself, borne in upon him from without, weighing as a 'burden' on his spirit, and only imperfectly assimilated by his own understanding. In this respect the superiority of the New Testament revelation stands out in bold relief. An older writer, Dr. P. Fairbairn, calls attention to this distinction in his work on *Prophecy*. 'To some extent,' he says, 'indeed, though very imperfectly as compared with Christ, the apostles shared in this higher standing and freer communion to such an extent as to form a marked distinction between them and the prophets of the earlier dispensation. For, excepting on a few special occasions, they never appear to have received revelations in trance or vision; and, like men habitually replenished with the Spirit, they spoke and wrote as if the Lord Himself spoke and wrote in them.'[1] This has an important bearing on the question of inspiration, for it is precisely this more perfect interpenetration of the apostles with the Spirit which, in the eyes of many, casts doubt on their possession of the Spirit in any peculiar degree at all. Many who would not question

[1] *Op. cit.* p. 11. Cf. *e.g.* 1 Thess. ii. 13.

that the Old Testament prophets were the recipients of revelations transcending their natural faculties, are yet disposed to attribute everything in the apostolic writings to the private thoughts and speculations of their authors, and leave no room for anything of the nature of authoritative revelation. Yet surely the position of the apostle in the economy of revelation is higher than that of the prophet, and the New Testament is not inferior in fulness of inspiration to the Old.

III. Forms of Biblical Revelation.

Revelation is *objective,* and likewise, it has been seen, *internal.* It has, besides, its higher and lower forms, the study of which helps to throw light on its nature and supernatural origin. Prophecy has been named as the highest form of Old Testament revelation. But attention may first be given to its earlier and lower forms,—those which lead up to the richer developments, and, in part, are involved in the latter.

Only a brief reference is necessary to certain modes of revelation—not, however, the earliest,—to which analogies are found in other religions. Such, *e.g.,* is the use of the 'lot,' which appears frequently in the Bible. Divination, indeed, or the attempt to discover the divine will, or forecast the future, by means of omens (cf. Ezek. xxi. 21), or other arbitrary signs, is everywhere sternly prohibited.[1] But a religious character is ascribed to the lot.[2] Examples of its use on solemn occasions are seen in the

[1] Lev. xix. 26, 31; Deut. xviii. 10-14. [2] Prov. xvi. 33.

detection of Achan,[1] the partition of Canaan,[2] the election of Saul,[3] in the New Testament, in the choosing of Matthias.[4] Probably akin to the lot was the mysterious 'Urim and Thummim' of the High Priest.[5] This humble means of giving guidance on critical occasions, God, in His condescension, permitted and made use of: the reality of the divine oracle being guaranteed by its fulfilment.[6]

Of modes or forms of divine revelation in the stricter sense the following may be distinguished.

1. The lowest form of special revelation recognised in Scripture is the *dream*. It is not implied that dreams generally, then, any more than now, were indications of the divine will. 'A dream cometh with multitude of business.'[7] 'Dreamer' is a term of reproach.[8] Dreams are put in a low grade in the Biblical revelations. A prophet is not allowed to authenticate himself only by dreams.[9] In special cases, however, God employed the dreaming state as a vehicle for His revelations. Generally it was persons who were not ordinarily or properly organs of revelation who received communications in this way—secular personages,

[1] Josh. vii. 14 ff.
[2] Josh. xiii. 6; xiv. 2.
[3] 1 Sam. x. 20-22.
[4] Acts, i. 26.
[5] Ex. xxviii. 30; Deut. xxxiii. 8, etc. The precise nature of the priestly oracle is disputed. On Egyptian analogies, cf. Oehler, *Theol. of O. T.* (E. T.), i. p. 319. Oehler remarks: 'These methods of inquiring into the divine will retire into the background the more prophecy is unfolded' (p. 320).
[6] Thus in the cases of Achan and Saul, as above; in the history of David, 1 Sam. xxiii. 2, 4, 11, 12, etc.
[7] Eccles. v. 3.
[8] Gen. xxxvii. 19.
[9] Deut. xiii. 2-5; Jer. xxiii. 28, etc.

heathen kings, etc. (*e.g.*, Abimelech,[1] Laban,[2] Joseph,[3] Pharaoh's butler and baker,[4] Pharaoh himself,[5] Nebuchadnezzar;[6] in the New Testament, Joseph,[7] the Magi[8]). The dream in a few of these cases does not interpret itself, but has to be interpreted by another (Joseph, Daniel). There is analogy for this mode of revelation, in some degree, in the natural phenomena of dreams; for it seems undeniable that in the sleeping state the soul is sometimes laid bare to the invisible world in a way that it is not in the waking condition.[9] In accordance with this natural basis, there is always a subjective or psychological side to revelations through dreams which imparts to them their special colouring. Pharaoh's dreams, *e.g.*, reflect the conditions of the Nile.[10]

2. Akin to the dream, though of a much higher character, is the *vision*,[11] frequently employed as a

1 Gen. xx. 3, 6.
2 Gen. xxxi. 24.
3 Gen. xxxvii. 5. Joseph's dreams were those of secular pre-eminence.
4 Gen. xl. 5.
5 Gen. xli. 1 ff.
6 Dan. ii. 1 ff.
7 Matt. i. 20; ii. 13, 19.
8 Matt. ii. 12.

9 Well-authenticated cases exist of impressions, presentiments, perceptions of things distant, even of prevision, in the sleeping state, which go beyond the limits of explanation by mere coincidence. The unusual powers manifested in somnambulism are familiar. Cf. the publications of the Society for Psychical Research; Myers's *Human Personality*, etc.

10 The dream is regarded as a peculiarity of the E document in the Pentateuch. On this, cf. *Prob. of the O. T.*, p. 233. Wellhausen infers from Gen. xxxviii. 19, that J also must have related Joseph's dream. The predominance of the dream in E sections may be connected with the fact that in the cases of Abimelech, Laban, Pharaoh, etc., God appears in His general character as the God of providence.

11 The words used for vision are מַרְאָה (*e.g.*, Num. xii. 6) or חִזָּיוֹן (2 Sam. vii. 17; Job, iv. 13, etc.), but more commonly חָזוֹן (Is. i. 1, etc.).

form of revelation. In Jacob's vision at Bethel it is said that Jacob 'dreamed,' but the narrative has more the character associated with vision.[1] Vision, however, was not necessarily, or even commonly, in sleep. It may be described as an abnormal state of consciousness, the effect of God's Spirit, in which the mind is supernaturally elevated, and things are seen and heard which would not be seen or heard in the ordinary state. The 'eyes are opened.'[2] The veil is drawn aside which divides seen and unseen, and there is an apprehension of supersensible realities. On its human side, the vision is a *subjective* phenomenon, that is, the things seen and heard are not there as outward facts, at least in the form in which they are perceived (the form is often symbolical), but are presented to the inner eye or ear. Yet it is a true presentation from the spiritual world.

It is obvious that, psychologically and otherwise, the phenomena of vision present many difficulties not easy to resolve. The things presented in vision, like all inner phenomena, take on a mental or imaginative character, yet are the means through which, in sight and sound, a divine revelation is conveyed. A typical example is the vision of Isaiah at the time of his call.[3] Jehovah is beheld seated on a throne, high and lifted up, in the temple, with the seraphim adoring. The foundations of the threshold of the building shake, and the house is filled with smoke. It is plain that, in this vision,

[1] Gen. xxviii. 12. Jacob falls asleep in the E document, and awakes in the J document.

[2] Cf. Num. xxii. 31; 2 Kings, vi. 17.

[3] Is. vi.

the prophet was not beholding an objective reality.[1] There was not really a throne set up in the temple, nor was the house actually filled with smoke. Yet through this vision the prophet received, as it was intended he should, a true impression of Jehovah's presence, majesty, and holiness, humbling him with a sense of his own unworthiness; then, in the words spoken, and the touching of his lips with the live coal from the altar, obtained the certainty of his divine call, consecration, and message to the people.

Vision is found as a form of revelation in both the Old Testament and the New. An early example is in the forming of the covenant with Abraham. Jacob had repeated visions.[2] As other instances, Moses and the elders of Israel had visions,[3] Balaam prophesied in vision,[4] Samuel's call was in vision.[5] Still vision is comparatively rare in the Old Testament till the prophetic period.[6] It is found in marked degree in the later prophets—Jeremiah, Ezekiel, and Zechariah, and is, naturally, the predominant feature in Apocalyptic prophecy (Daniel; in the New Testament, the Book of Revelation). In the New Testament we have the visions of Cornelius and Peter.[7] Paul also had 'visions and revelations of the Lord.'[8] The Apocalypse is wholly vision.

The place of vision in prophecy will be better considered when that form of revelation comes to

[1] Cf. John's vision of Christ in Rev. i.

[2] Gen. xlvi. 2 ff.; cf. xxviii. 10 ff.; xxxi. 11 ff. ('dream'); xxxv. 1, 9 ff.

[3] Ex. xxiv. 9 ff.; xxxiii. 18 ff.

[4] Num. xxiv. 3, 4 ff.

[5] 1 Sam. iii. 13.

[6] Vision is found in the ministries of Elijah and Elisha; in Amos, viii. 1 ff., etc. Isaiah's vision is referred to above.

[7] Acts, x. 3 ff., 9 ff.

[8] 2 Cor. xii. 1.

be directly treated. The view once held that all prophecy was uttered in a state of ecstasy must be set aside as out of harmony with the facts. If, as frequently happens, the name 'vision' is used to describe those prophecies in which, properly speaking, no vision occurs—*e.g.*, 'the vision of Isaiah the son of Amoz'[1]—this is to be explained by the usage of a time in which vision was, perhaps, the predominant form of prophecy; but is also intended to denote the fact of the exaltation, the supernatural origin, and the vividness—as of actual seeing—of the prophetic perception. For undoubtedly prophecy *was* in every case an elevation above the ordinary state of consciousness. More difficult is the question, how far the state called vision enters in narrative and prophecy into experiences which are not directly described as such. The burning bush beheld by Moses,[2] *e.g.*,—would that have been seen by any other eyes but his at that time and place? Possibly not; yet the 'glory of the Lord' appears so often in the narrative as an objective phenomenon—*e.g.*, in the pillar of cloud and fire—that it is reasonable to assume a real appearance at the bush also. The speaking of the ass of Balaam,[3] again—that subject which has caused so much concern—would that have been heard by the ear of any ordinary bystander? Or was it, as the context would suggest, an impression on Balaam's own mind? Still less is it easy to determine whether certain of the actions of the prophets which are related in the form of narrative—*e.g.*, Jeremiah's hiding of his girdle by the river Euphrates[4]—are to

[1] Is. i. 1.
[2] Ex. iii. 2.
[3] Num. xxii. 22-35.
[4] Jer. xiii 1-5.

be understood as literal transactions, or as events occurring in vision. The question is reserved to another chapter.

3. A third and exceptionally interesting form of revelation, belonging peculiarly to patriarchal and Mosaic times, is that through the *Angel of God*, or *Angel of Jehovah*. This is a form of revelation which stands by itself, and presents peculiarities which have given rise to much discussion. The fact that it belongs almost exclusively to the earlier period, when revelation was preponderatingly objective, shows that it is part of the original tradition, and not a reflection from later prophetic times, when revelation had a totally different form.

The peculiarity of revelation by the *Malach*, or Angel of Jehovah, is, that this angel appears as a divine messenger, yet constantly acts and speaks in a way which implies His identity with Jehovah. The doctrine of angels, it is to be remarked, is not one highly developed in the Pentateuch. When angels appear, as at Bethel and Mahanaim, it is collectively.[1] This angel, in any case, is not an ordinary angel, but stands in a peculiar nearness to Jehovah, represents Him, and, as far as words can do it, is identified with Him. The 'Angel of the Lord' (Jehovah) appears to Hagar, but He speaks to her as God;[2] and the next verse reads: 'And she called the name of the Lord that spake unto her, Thou art a God that seeth.'[3] Abraham extends hospitality to three travellers, one of whom is early identified with Jehovah, the omnipotent,[4]

[1] Gen. xxviii. 12; xxxii. 1, 2. The paucity of reference to angels is another mark of the early nature of the tradition.

[2] Gen. xvi. 10-12. [3] Ver. 13. [4] Gen. xviii. 13, 14.

the righteous,[1] the Judge of all the earth.[2] It is Jehovah who departs from Abraham after his intercession for Sodom.[3] The 'Angel of the Lord,' again, appears to Abraham on Moriah, and speaks as Jehovah.[4] It is evidently this same Angel with whom, as a man, Jacob wrestles, and obtains from Him, as God, the blessing.[5] In Gen. xlviii. 15, 16, God and the Angel are apparently identified. It is the 'Angel of the Lord' who reveals Himself to Moses at the bush as the God of the fathers, and as 'Jehovah' ('I Am').[6] 'Jehovah,' but elsewhere 'the Angel of God,' goes before the Israelites; and the people are warned not to provoke the Angel, for Jehovah's 'Name' is in Him.[8] It is unnecessary to deal with the later appearances, as to Joshua, Gideon, Manoah, etc.[9]

How, it is naturally asked, are such appearances to be understood? Different answers have been given.

1. One view held by many is that the *Malach* is a created angel, of high dignity, who represents God, and speaks in His name, as later is done by the prophets.[10] The analogy, however, does not hold. The prophets, indeed, speak for Jehovah in the first person, but they as clearly again distinguish themselves from their message and its Author. They usually preface their message with a 'Thus

[1] Ver. 19. [2] Ver. 25. [3] Ver. 33.
[4] Gen. xxii. 11 ff. [5] Gen. xxxi. 24-30; cf. Hos. xii. 4.
[6] Ex. iii. 6, 14. [7] Ex. xiii. 21; xiv. 19.
[8] Ex. xxiii. 20, 21.
[9] Josh. v. 13-15; Judg. vi. 11 ff.; xiii. 3 ff.; cf. Is. lxiii. 9; Zech. iii. 1; Mal. iii. 1 ff.
[10] Thus Augustine and other Fathers. In modern times, Hofmann, Kurtz, Delitzsch, etc.

saith Jehovah,' and no one dreams of identifying them with the Jehovah whose words they utter. But the *Malach* does not bring a message of this kind. He speaks in the first person, and in the course of the narrative we find that the speaker is directly interchanged with Jehovah, and is addressed as Jehovah.

2. A second view, accordingly, is that the *Malach* is not personally distinct from Jehovah, but is simply a *manifestation* of Jehovah Himself in the phenomenal world—an entrance into visibility for the immediate end of revelation—a direct *theophany*. This might be accepted, and answers well to certain of the passages, but fails to do justice to the fact that in most of the places—indeed, in the name itself—a distinction from Jehovah is implied as well as a seeming identity with Him.

3. The third view, therefore, usually held by those who reject the first, is that, in the *Malach*, we have indeed a manifestation of Jehovah, but of Jehovah in the form of *self-distinction*. The revelation through the Angel, in other words, points to a real distinction in the nature of God such as is associated in the New Testament with the idea of the Logos or Son. The *Malach*, on this view, is identified with the Word, or Son of God, who afterwards became incarnate in Christ. Many of the Fathers (Justin Martyr, Tertullian,[1] Irenaeus, etc.) adopt this interpretation of the theophanies. It is a view which has been held very widely in the Church.

The objection naturally taken to this third interpretation is that it seems to read back into the early

[1] Tertullian speaks of the theophanies as 'rehearsals' of the incarnation.

stages of revelation the New Testament doctrine of the Trinity. In reply it may be said that the question is really not so much one of doctrine as of the interpretation of historical facts. We cannot, indeed, legitimately read back New Testament ideas into these early narratives, as if the writers possessed, or intended to convey, a developed doctrine of the Trinity. But it is not inadmissible, in interpreting God's earlier revelations, to use any light that comes to us from the later; and if later revelation makes clear to us, as it does, a real self-distinction in God, there exists no reason why we should not avail ourselves of the aid of that truth here. Oehler seems to come very near the essence of the matter when he sums up by saying, that 'the *Malach* was a self-presentation of Jehovah entering into the sphere of the creature, which is one in essence with Jehovah, and is yet again distinct from Him.'[1] The appearances of the *Malach* may thus reasonably be held to be an adumbration, and in part an anticipation, of the later incarnation of the Son.[2]

The other forms of theophany in the Old Testament, as in the fire at the bush, the pillar of fire, the glory at the tabernacle, etc., are not always to be distinguished from the *Malach*, but are, as already seen forms of His manifestation.

[1] *Op. cit.*, i. p. 193.

[2] Even H. Schultz, who takes a mediating view, allows: 'There is undoubtedly in the Angel of God something of that which Christian theology means to express by the doctrine of the Logos' (*O. T. Theol.* (E.T.), ii. p. 223). Delitzsch, who favours the idea of a created angel (*New Com. on Genesis*, on ch. xvi. 7, etc.), still holds that 'the angelologies of God were a prefiguration of His Christophany' (ii. p. 21).

CHAPTER V

FORMS OF REVELATION, *continued*: PROPHECY—DIFFICULTIES OF REVELATION

THREE forms of divine revelation have been adverted to—dream, vision, and theophany, or revelation through the *Malach* or 'Angel of Jehovah.' It is now necessary to speak of *prophecy*—the highest and most important of all forms of Old Testament revelation.

I. NATURE OF PROPHECY.

1. Prophecy is a phenomenon peculiar to Israel. Heathenism has divination, oracles, manticism;[1] and it has been seen that divine impulse and guidance are not wholly to be refused to the wise men and teachers of other peoples.[2] But in Israel alone we have the spectacle of a succession of men, speaking with full consciousness in the name of a holy and righteous God, maintaining a lofty and continuous testimony to His will and purpose, and, amidst the greatest revolutions in outward affairs, unerringly interpreting His providence in its bearing on the ends of His Kingdom—testimony and

[1] On the phenomena in heathenism, cf. again Orelli, *op. cit.* (E.T.), pp. 13 ff. According to Plato (in *Timaeus*), the μάντις was the ecstatic utterer of an oracle; the προφήτης the sober-minded interpreter of the oracle of the former.

[2] See above, p. 57.

prediction finding their fulfilment in the advent, work, and spiritual Kingdom of the New Testament Redeemer.[1]

Prophecy has its analogy in human *genius*. Some, accordingly, have sought its explanation in that gift of geniality, of presentiment, of divining intuition, with which certain nobler natures are undeniably endowed;[2] others see in it only a heightening of that spiritual faculty which, through faith in God and righteousness, discerns the sure issues of good or evil, wise or foolish, conduct, to which the multitudes are blind.[3] But while a basis of natural endowment, fitting him for his vocation, is always presupposed in the prophet, this alone falls far short of accounting for the kind of prophecy we have in the Old Testament. The clearness, elevation, certainty, decision, above all, the spiritual content of Old Testament prophecy, present features which every naturalistic theory, and even general spiritual illumination, fail to explain. The element of prediction in prophecy stands by itself. But in their ministry as a whole the prophets knew with perfect clearness that the vision they received, the word of God which came to them with overmastering certainty, the message given them for the

[1] After careful examination, Orelli says: 'We come to the conclusion that no phenomenon analogous to Biblical prophecy, even in form, is anywhere to be found in the world of nations' (*op. cit.*, p. 24).

[2] On these views, cf. Oehler, *Theol. of O. T.*, ii. pp. 340 ff. Giesebrecht, more recently, explains prophecy from a 'gift of *Ahnungsvermögen*' with which the prophet is endowed—heightened, however, by the action of the Spirit of God (*Die Berufgabung der Alttest. Propheten*, pp. 74, 76, 77, etc.).

[3] Thus Ewald, and many.

people, were not the products of their own thoughts, but had their source in the divine revealing Spirit.

2. A probable etymology of the Hebrew words for 'prophet' and 'prophecy' connects them with a root meaning 'to bubble.'[1] Hence the prophet would be one in whom the divine inspiration bubbles up from heart to lip. Whatever the etymology, the general sense of the word 'prophet' is not doubtful. The prophet is one who speaks for God to men: he is, as Augustine calls him, *enuntiator verborum dei hominibus*. This function of the prophet is defined in Deut. xviii. 18: 'I will raise them up a prophet from among their brethren like unto thee; and I will put my words in his mouth, and he shall speak unto them all that I shall command him.'[2] The expressions employed to describe the prophetic state are such as imply direct inspiration and revealing action. The Spirit of God comes on the prophets; falls on them; 'the hand of Jehovah' is strong upon them;[3] they perceive, as with the force of bodily perception, facts or truths presented to their minds;[4] they receive a 'word' of God, and experience an irresistible constraint to utter it. The recurring formula is, 'the word of God came'

[1] נָבִיא (prophet) from נָבָא (cognate to נָבַע), used only in Niphal and Hithpael (to prophesy). The Niphal form perhaps suggests passivity.

[2] In this sense Aaron is given to be a 'prophet' to Moses, *i.e.*, to speak for him (Ex. iv. 10-17; vii. 1).

[3] Is. viii. 11; Jer. xv. 17; Ezek. i. 3; iii. 22; xxxvii. 1, etc.

[4] Cf. Orelli, *op. cit.*, p. 5: 'The essential element to be maintained in prophecy is, that it *sees* its contents before announcing them. . . . The contents of prophecy are, consequently, not something thought out, inferred, hoped, or feared by the prophets, but something directly perceived.'

to one or another;[1] and this word, which the prophets distinguish quite clearly from their own thoughts and desires, they unhesitatingly proclaim as the word of Jehovah, and take their stand upon its truth and the certainty of its fulfilment.

3. It was formerly a not uncommon conception, borrowed from Philo and the early Church, that the prophets received their oracles in a *state of ecstasy*, in which their own minds were purely passive.[2] The element of truth to be recognised in this view is, that prophecy implied an unusual and exalted state of consciousness, and *sometimes* took the form of ecstasy or vision. Is. vi. was before given as an example, and there are many others. But that this was the only or invariable—even the principal—way of receiving divine communications, the whole history of prophecy refutes. Nothing is plainer than that, in all the higher forms of prophecy, the prophets retained their consciousness and full command of their faculties. Not only were their natural powers not suppressed: they were raised to the fullest activity of which they were capable. 'It has been justly remarked,' says Riehm, 'that from the 40th to the 66th chapters of Isaiah, and, indeed, in most of the predictions of Isaiah, Jeremiah, Ezekiel, Hosea, Micah, and others, there is no trace of a description of pictures seen in ecstasy.'[3] Even where the word 'vision' is employed, it is often, as already explained, used in a general sense.

1 Joel, i. 1; Jer. i. 4; xi. 13; Ezek. i. 3; Zech. i. 1; Mal. i. 1, etc.

2 Hengstenberg at first defended this view, but afterwards considerably modified it.

3 *Messianic Prophecy* (E.T.), p. 17. On a possible qualification of this statement, in respect of vision, see below.

II. Prophecy in its Historic Relations.

1. It is usual to connect the *beginnings* of prophecy with Samuel, and appeal is made in support of this to 1 Sam. ix. 9: 'He that is now called a prophet was beforetime called a seer.'[1] This usage, however, can only have application to a particular time ('The word of the Lord was precious in those days; there was no frequent vision'[2]), or to official designation. Biblical history knows perfectly well of an earlier prophecy.[3] Still, prophecy in the more official and continuous sense did begin with Samuel and his prophetic companies, and continued thereafter uninterruptedly till after the return from exile. But there is here also development. Samuel himself stands from the first on the higher plane of prophecy. His call is followed by a calm, equable development.[4] But in the circle around him the action of the spirit of prophecy is marked by the physical excitement which denotes a lower stage.[5] The loftier height of prophecy is again reached, at a great crisis in the history of Israel, by Elijah and Elisha, who, however, are still acting, rather than teaching or writing, prophets. Finally, with Amos and Hosea (possibly with Joel) begins the series of writing prophets, who continue till Malachi.

[1] The term 'seer' denotes a gift analogous to clairvoyance. It does not follow that this was a gift in the prophet's own power, or was exercised about every trifling matter on which people sought to consult him. The prophet saw as God gave him to see (cf. 1 Sam. ix. 15), and his answers had reference, not to any or every kind of events, but, as in Saul's case, to those which had a bearing on God's Kingdom.

[2] 1 Sam. iii. 1.

[3] Thus Abraham, Moses, Balaam, Deborah, etc.

[4] 1 Sam. iii. 19-21.

[5] 1 Sam. x. 11-13; xix. 20-24.

Not till the eve of Christ's appearance is the voice of prophecy again heard (Zacharias, Simeon, John the Baptist).

2. It is now generally recognised as a serious mistake of older writers to identify prophecy so *exclusively* as they did with prediction, and to regard this in the light of an external seal attached to the prophet's message. It was really in the prophet's *message to his own times* that the essence of his prophecy lay. The prophet was in the first instance a messenger to his own age and people: the message he brought was one called forth by the needs of his age, and in form and substance was adapted to these needs. It does not follow, because of this, that it was a message *only* for his own time, and did not embody a revelation of God of universal import, fitted to take its place in the general organism of revelation. Prophecy was instinct with germinal ideas; with promises, hopes, admonitions, threatenings; with abundant predictions of nearer or more remote events, in their revelations to God's Kingdom. The predictive element will be referred to after. The chief thing to be observed at present is the intimate relation which prophecy always sustains to the historical conditions out of which it springs. This historical setting can never be ignored, if prophecy is to be understood. The marvel of the prophecy of Amos, *e.g.*, can only be realised when the outward prosperity, yet inward decadence, of the reign of a Jeroboam II. in Israel are kept in view; the plaint of Hosea, when one sees the eagles of Assyria [1] gathering to make their prey of doomed Samaria; the magnifi-

[1] Hos. viii. 1.

cence of Isaiah's faith and courage, when one places himself in the midst of the politics and perils of Judah in the age of Hezekiah; the patriotism of Jeremiah, or prayer of Habakkuk, when one hears the resistless tread of the approaching Chaldæan armies. The exile must be remembered in order to the right apprehension of the visions of Ezekiel, or of the consolations and hopes of the oracles of Is. xl. ff.

III. Tests of True Prophecy.

1. But were the prophets under no hallucination when they ascribed, as they so confidently did, their messages and forecasts of the future, even of far-distant events, to the voice of God within them? That is a fair question to ask. Scripture knows of a false prophecy as well as of a true. The prophets themselves had to wage a continual warfare with others whom they denounced as deceivers.[1] But may not these so-called 'false prophets' be, as some have contended, as true as the others, and may the conflict not be only one of rival prophetic camps? Where is the test?

The prophecy of the Bible offers such *tests*—tests, however, which, like those applicable to Christ Himself, presuppose spiritual discernment in those employing them. It is not enough that the prophets *say* that they have the word of God; that they proclaim their possession of the Spirit; that they adduce dreams.[2] Four tests in particular may be instanced:—

[1] Mic. iii. 16; Jer. xxiii. 9 ff.; Ezek. xiii 2 ff., etc. Cf. A. B. Davidson, *O. T. Prophecy*, ch. xvii., 'The False Prophets.'

[2] Jer. xxiii. 28. It is not enough even that the prophet works miracles, Deut. xiii. 1-3.

(1) The claim of the prophet was supported, first, by his own *known character* as a man of God. Genuine prophecy implied a spiritual receptivity. For the reception of God's word there was needed a preparation of soul,[1] a devout, earnest, deeply-religious nature, anxious and waiting on God to know His will.[2] The prophets of Israel were one and all men of uprightness and sincerity, whose whole spirit, conduct, manner of life, and freedom from interested motives, placed them above the suspicion of being wilful deceivers or self-deceived.

(2) Character, however, was not the only test. The word of the prophet was supported, further, by its own *internal power*. The word spoken was in large measure a self-attesting word; a word instinct with the Spirit of holiness; suited to the time and need of the nation; to that extent one which could be verified by the intelligence and conscience of those that heard it.[3] As originating from God, it was a word bearing on the ends of God's Kingdom, and directed to the furtherance of these ends.

(3) It was a special test of a true word of prophecy that it *fitted into the organism of revelation*; in other words, that it cohered with, and did not subvert or contradict, the scheme of revelation so far as it had already gone, It is emphatically laid down, as in Deut. xiii. 1-3, that the prophetic word must not contradict fundamental truth, or previous words of God, but must establish and develop them.

[1] Balaam and Saul may be cited as instances to the contrary. But neither could have been accepted as a prophet in Israel.

[2] Cf. Hab. ii. 1-4.

[3] Cf. Paul, 2 Cor. iv. 2: 'By the manifestation of the truth commending ourselves to every man's conscience in the sight of God.'

(4) Finally, a test of the word of prophecy was its *fulfilment*. In true prophecy there was generally some promise, warning, or declaration of God as to what was going to happen, and the prophet's standing was based on the fulfilment of that word.[1] The fulfilment of prophecy, accordingly, is often appealed to in evidence of its truth.[2]

2. Such being the nature of genuine prophecy, it is plain that the prophetic office was not one which any individual could take to himself. Neither genius, nor spiritual disposition, nor training by others, could of itself make a man a prophet. The prophet was made so by *the call of* God, and, when that call came, it did so in a manner about which there could be no mistake. Examples suggest themselves in the cases of Moses,[3] Samuel,[4] Amos,[5] Isaiah,[6] Jeremiah.[7] The disciples of the prophets in the prophetic 'schools' or 'guilds' were not all prophets, or received the name only in courtesy. The schools might prepare a congenial soil for the spirit of prophecy; but the call was not confined to the members of these fraternities. 'I was no prophet,' says Amos, 'neither was I a prophet's son; but I was a herdsman, and a dresser of sycamore-trees; and Jehovah took me from following the flock, and Jehovah said unto me, Go, prophesy unto my people Israel.'[8] The prophet to

[1] Deut. xviii. 21, 22. The test as given in these verses is a negative one: 'How shall we know the word which Jehovah hath not spoken?' Non-fulfilment was a test of false prophecy; but, if the prophet preached idolatry, even fulfilment, or miracle, could not authenticate his word (Deut. xiii. 1-3).

[2] Is. xxxiv. 16; xli. 21 ff.; xlii. 9; xliii. 9.

[3] Ex. iii. 11 ff. [4] 1 Sam. ii. 4 ff. [5] Amos vii. 14 ff.

[6] Is. vi. [7] Jer. i. 4 ff. [8] Amos vii. 14, 15.

whom the call came may not have expected or desired it; on the contrary, he may have been conscious of his utter unfitness, and may have resisted it till he felt that he dare not resist further. Jeremiah is a case in point here.[1] With the call in every case came the equipment and the definite message; the prophet was supernaturally endowed.

IV. Prediction in Prophecy.

Discussion has gathered in an especial way round *the element of prediction* in Biblical prophecy, because here is an element in which the presence of the supernatural must either be acknowledged, or the prophecy itself be explained away or denied.

1. There can be little question as to the *claims* of the prophets to utter predictions of the future; and nearly as little as to the impossibility of explaining these predictions, on the assumption of their genuineness, out of mere natural foresight. The method is still open of endeavouring to show that the predictions in question were not written till after the event; are late additions or interpolations; or, when admitted to be genuine, that they were not really fulfilled. Unfortunately, the chief predictions, as, *e.g.*, those of Amos of the approaching Assyrian invasion, and Captivity of Israel;[2] those of Hosea and Isaiah of the fall of Samaria;[3] Isaiah's prediction of the deliverance of Jerusalem from Sennacherib;[4] Jeremiah's prophecy of the seventy years' captivity and subsequent return,[5] etc., are

[1] Jer. i. 4 ff.
[2] Amos v. 27; vii. 11, 17, etc.
[3] Hos. viii., etc.; Is. xxviii., etc.
[4] Is. xxxvii. 26-36.
[5] Jer. xxv. 11, 12.

of a nature which, except by uncritical violence, can neither be expunged from the text, nor got rid of as unfulfilled. They stand as types of a kind of prediction which pervades Biblical prophecy from beginning to end. When it is objected that to introduce supernatural prediction is to put Hebrew prophecy on the level of 'soothsaying,' it is overlooked that prediction, in the prophets, is never brought in as a wonder on its own account, but always in its bearing on the ends of God's Kingdom.[1] It is never a mere portent, but has its place in the unfolding of God's purpose for the world. A peculiar form of predictive prophecy is the *Apocalyptic*, as in Daniel and the Revelation of John, in which future events and crises in the history of God's Kingdom are set forth under the veil of symbol. Some of the symbols are interpreted, while others remain enigmatic.[2]

2. Of chief interest, in this connection, from the Christian standpoint, is the long series of predictions, which helped to create the expectation of the Messiah and of His future Kingdom—*Messianic* prophecy, as it is wont to be termed. This line of prophecy, ranging from the first promise in Eden, through the promises to Abraham and those of the Mosaic age, the prophecies connecting the future King with the tribe of Judah and the house of David, the promises of the New Covenant, of the gift of the Spirit, of the admission of the Gentiles,

[1] On this point, and the whole question of predictive prophecy, see *Problem of the O. T.*, pp. 454 ff.

[2] Apocalypse in Scripture is not to be explained out of current Jewish apocalyptic tendencies; conversely, Jewish Apocalypse is to be explained from the Biblical models.

to the great culminating prophecies of the Servant of Jehovah—humbled, atoning, yet finally triumphant—founds the expectation of a perfect Prophet, perfect Priest, and perfect King—One whose Personality, as in the Immanuel prophecy,[1] breaks the bounds of mere humanity, and only finds its fulfilment in the Christ of the New Testament.

V. Interpretation of Prophecy.

1. Difficulties, naturally, often of no small magnitude, arise in connection with the *interpretation* of a body of prophecy so vast, complex, and sometimes obscure, as that transmitted to us in the books of the Old Covenant. Here also arise questions of date, authorship, text,—such questions, *e.g.*, as to how far Is. xl.-lxvi. is a work of the exile, or is itself composite, or is, to a greater extent than modern scholars are willing to recognise, the work of Isaiah himself;[2] or whether Daniel, in its present form, or entirely, is a work of the Maccabean age. These critical questions cannot be gone into here. The solution of the difficulties of interpretation are mostly to be sought for in a closer examination of the peculiarities of prophecy itself:—in observation of the ideal element which necessarily enters into predictions of the more distant future; of the inevitable clothing of the representations of that future in

[1] Is. vii. 14; viii. 8; ix. 6, 7.

[2] It is not always considered that, as shown by Jer. xxvi. 17-19, there was an expectation and prediction of a destruction of Jerusalem, and captivity of the people to Babylon, in the days of Isaiah and Micah (Mic. iii. 12; iv. 10; Is. vi. 11, 12; xxxix. 6, 7), though on account of the repentance of king and people, as Jeremiah tells, the judgment was postponed.

forms borrowed from the present; of the lack of perspective in the grouping together of events of the consummation; and, not least, of the *conditional* element in prophecy, leaving room for change in the mode of fulfilment under altered conditions.[1] The one thing ever certain to the prophet's mind is the consummation itself of the future Kingdom of God—the shattering of all earthly opposition to God's purposes, and realisation of the divine will in a new heaven and a new earth!

2. A word may be said here on a question already raised: How far a *visionary element* enters into prophetic descriptions which do not, on their face, bear this character? The principle of vision has sometimes, perhaps, been carried to an extreme, as when, *e.g.*, Hosea's marriage to Gomer has been translated into a visionary transaction.[2] But other sections of prophecy, into which, as here, no moral problem enters, force the question upon us. Such instances, *e.g.*, as Jeremiah's long journey to the Euphrates to hide his girdle, and his second journey, after many days, to recover it;[3] Isaiah's walking 'naked and barefoot' for three years for a sign and wonder concerning Egypt;[4] Ezekiel's lying on his side for three hundred and ninety days before the drawing of the siege of Jerusalem on a tile,[5] etc. There are difficulties on any view; but the literal interpretation of these commands almost involves incredibilities. Those scholars who find it natural

[1] These points are treated of in *Prob. of O. T.*, pp. 460 ff. Cf. Orelli, *op. cit.*, pp. 50 ff.

[2] Thus Hengstenberg, Keil, etc.

[3] Jer. xiii. 1-11.

[4] Is. xx.

[5] Ezek. iv. 1-18. On this class of transactions generally, cf. P. Fairbairn, *Prophecy*, pp. 124 ff., and his Appendix, pp. 508 ff.

to place a parabolic interpretation on Jonah's 'three days and three nights' in the belly of the fish, should hardly shrink from granting that the conditions in the foregoing instances are satisfied by a transaction in vision.

VI. Difficulties in Old Testament Revelation.

It will be proper, before leaving the subject of revelation in the Old Testament, to glance briefly at the *difficulties* which undoubtedly arise in the consideration of this revelation, especially in its relation to the teaching of the New Testament. The class of difficulties in view are not those connected with miracle—these will be dealt with in another chapter—or those arising from supposed conflicts of the Bible with science. The latter give little concern, once it is recognised that the Bible is not a text-book of physical science, anticipatory of the discoveries of the nineteenth and twentieth centuries. Few people are any longer disturbed by the acceptance of the Copernican theory of the heavens, or the knowledge of the long duration of the ages of geology; the theory of evolution, now commonly accepted in principle, has undergone modifications which remove most of the aspects of conflict between it and the theistic and Christian view of the world; the older statements made as to the enormous antiquity and primitive barbarism of man, are undergoing considerable revision; while the scriptural (rather the Ussherian) chronology is, on its side, discovered to need, and to admit of, a corresponding extension. It will be difficult for any one to show that the ideas about God, man's sin, man's need, the dependence of the world on God as its Creator and Ruler, contained in the Bible, are in any real conflict with what a sober science teaches.[1]

1. The difficulties intended are those *inherent in the revelation itself* which may be thought to stamp it as something *inferior*, and unworthy of the God of the New Testament. Among these may be named the primitive and *naïve* conceptions of God and His actions found especially in the earlier portions of the Bible (anthropomorphisms, as God 'coming down' to see, repenting, etc.); the defective morality of Biblical characters (*e.g.*, Jacob, Samson, David); the sanction given to such institutions as polygamy, divorce, blood-revenge, slavery, which the Christian conscience condemns; chiefly, perhaps, the severity of the codes of justice, the commands for the extermination of whole tribes and peoples (Amalekites, Canaanites), acts like the hewing of Agag in pieces before the Lord. The old Gnostics, founding on these and like imperfections in the Old Testament revelation, boldly ascribed the whole to an inferior Deity—the Demiurge. Bishop Butler, in modern times, would urge our ignorance of the scheme of revelation as a whole, and point to analogies in God's natural government, raising similar difficulties.

2. Several of the above-named difficulties seem adequately met by appeal to the idea of *progress* in revelation—an idea to which Butler in his *Analogy* does not do the justice it demands. Revelation is not complete all at once. If the light with which it starts is dim, it grows clearer as the ages advance.

[1] See more fully in the author's *Bible Under Trial*, ch. ix., 'Oppositions of Science,' and *God's Image in Man*; also below, p. 168.

The world into which it comes is one deeply sunk in sin, and in the evils which sin brings with it. Revelation has to take up man as it finds him, with his crude conceptions, his childlike modes of thought and expression, his defective moral ideas and social institutions, and has to make the best of him it can. Imperfect conditions have to be borne with for the time, while germs of truth and principles are implanted which, in their development, gradually throw off the defective forms, and evolve higher.

In no other way, it should be evident, could God carry on the government of the world. In no other way, even yet, can Christian nations legislate and act, in the full light of Christ's teaching, than by patient toleration of much that is avowedly defective and sinful, till what is better has had time to grow. The wisdom of this method of revelation is seen in its results. Polygamy, *e.g.*, is contradicted, as Jesus says,[1] by the first principles of the Bible's teaching on man, yet had to be tolerated as a defective social institution till higher conceptions could be evolved. But by Christ's time polygamy had nearly disappeared. Divorce was tolerated, we are told, for the hardness of the people's hearts,[2] and was destined in time to give place to a higher law. Blood-revenge was checked by the law of the refuge-cities, and gradually died out with the growth of settled order and of regular legal procedure. Slavery similarly was counterworked by the higher ideas of man in Israel's religion, and the generally beneficent spirit of its legislation, and in Christ's time had likewise largely disappeared.

[1] Matt. xix. 3-9. [2] Matt. xix. 8.

3. A very real difficulty is presented in the *unsparing use of the sword* in war, and the commanded *extermination of whole populations*, as in the case of the Canaanites. Was this really God's command ? Criticism has a simple and plausible way of disposing of these difficulties, viz., by denying that they belong to revelation at all. The writers of the Bible, it is said, attribute to Jehovah their own defective, semi-barbarous conceptions. Hence they unhesitatingly ascribe to God such enormities as the slaughter of the Canaanites, or the hewing in pieces of Agag. The fault of the explanation is that it seems to remove the foundations of the revelation altogether; so in reality creates more difficulties than it resolves. For, if anything seems clear in Bible history, it is that the action of the Israelites in taking possession of Canaan, and making a clearance of its inhabitants, was not the outcome of their own thoughts or designs—they are blamed for not doing it more thoroughly—but was the result of direct commands of God, in fulfilment of His promises to their fathers. There is not a suggestion anywhere, in Old Testament or New, that this is not the true reading of events.[1] What is to be said of it ?

In this connection, again, the *progressiveness of revelation* counts for something. The usages and customs of ancient warfare are to be remembered. It is to be borne in mind also that the cases of the Canaanites, and of other tribes and individuals put under the 'ban,' are exceptional. Extermination was not the rule in Israelitish warfare, though generally war, even internal strife, was

[1] Cf. Acts vii. 4, 5; xiii. 19.

fierce enough. The laws of warfare are humane and merciful compared with those of other nations.[1] They give no sanction whatever to the frightful tortures—the impalings, flayings, blindings, mutilations—depicted on Assyrian and Babylonian monuments. But chiefly, extermination, where commanded, has always an *ethical reason*. If the Canaanites were condemned, it was because, after long patience of God, the cup of their iniquities was full to overflowing.[2] 'After all,' says Ottley, quoting Westcott, 'the Canaanites were put under the ban, "not for false belief, but for vile actions."'[3] Nor was there any partiality in this. To quote what has been said elsewhere: 'The sword of the Israelite is, after all, only a more acute form of the problem that meets us in the providential employment of the sword of the Assyrian, the Chaldean, and the Roman, to inflict the judgment of God on Israel itself.'[4]

VII. Wider Considerations.

1. The question may be looked at in a wider light. The whole spirit of the Old Covenant is, on the judicial side, in comparison with the New, one of *marked severity*. It was an economy in which 'every transgression and disobedience received a just recompense of reward.'[5] Yet it is a mistake not to recognise that an awful severity, as well as a long-suffering goodness, belongs to the God of the New Testament also. If law veils grace in the old economy, grace must not be permitted to blind us

[1] Cf. Deut. xii.
[2] Gen. xv. 16; Lev. viii. 24-30.
[3] *Aspects of the O. T.*, p. 179.
[4] *Prob. of O. T.*, pp. 471-2.
[5] Heb. ii. 2.

to the sternness of God's holiness under the Gospel. God is still 'the Judge,' [1] and very terrible are the words used of His judgments on evil-doers who resist His mercy. 'The day of wrath and revelation of the righteous judgment of God . . . wrath and indignation, tribulation and anguish, upon every soul of man that worketh evil.' [2] Jesus is the revelation of the love of God; but what terrible words of doom fall sometimes from His lips.[3] The God of the Christian revelation, we early discover, is not a God who cannot both look upon and do things very terrible. 'He that spared not His own Son, but delivered Him up [to a cross] for us all.' [4]

2. To this also, so far to apply Butler's argument, corresponds the revelation of God in *nature*. If we are not to fall into dualism, it is the same God whom Christ revealed who must be acknowledged to work and rule in the natural creation. But what terrible things—famines, blights, pestilences, the sweeping away of whole populations by earthquake, fire, flood—are to be witnessed there? Or in providence, —what permission of tyranny, crime, oppression, where a word, it might be thought, would smite the oppressor in the dust? Yet God is silent. These are the enigmas of God's natural government. Is anything in the Old Testament harder?

3. The argument of Butler may be applied with even enhanced force to *the 'modern' objector* who declaims against the character and commands of the God of the Old Testament. It changes the form of the problem, but does not alter the essence of it, if,

[1] 1 Pet. i. 17. [2] Rom. ii. 5-9.
[3] Matt. xiii. 41-2; xxiv. 50-1; xxv. 41, 46; Luke xix. 27, etc.
[4] Rom. viii. 32.

with the modern school, for 'revelation' we use the word 'evolution.' What is the Power behind evolution? God. But who is to interpret God to us for the purposes of religion? If Professor Bousset, in his *What is Religion?*, or Professor G. B. Foster, in his *Finality of the Christian Religion*, are to be trusted, it is Jesus. Here are Bousset's words; 'We hold fast with all our power to the faith of the Gospel in a personal, heavenly Father. . . . We lift our hands in prayer and say, "Our Father in Heaven". . . All this; God the Father, life in accordance with His will spent in joyful work for the service of the world, forgiveness of sins, and eternal hope—all this hangs together, and is crystallised in perfect clearness in the Person of our Lord Jesus.' [1]

But see now the picture which is given us of this God in nature, history, and religion.

In nature:—'We carry this idea of faith into our modern knowledge, into our representation of God. . . . God is to us the Eternal, the All-Powerful One, who is potent in the vast, starry world and in the eternities of time and space, before which thought grows dizzy—potent alike in the eternally insignificant things and in the eternally great things. He is the God whose garment is the iron law of Nature, which hides Him from human eyes in a thick husk which cannot be torn off; who, in accordance with the terrible law of the struggle for existence, leads His creatures upwards into a world of moral, individual freedom; who surrounds us with His existence as with a dizzy abyss. And clinging to the hand of Jesus we venture to plunge into the abyss.' [2]

[1] *Op. cit.*, pp. 294-5, 298. [2] P. 294.

In religion :—Man begins, as we saw, as a savage, with hideous rites of immolation, human sacrifice, cannibalism ; he mounts upwards through low stages of society (the matriarchate, totemism, polygamy) to tribal and national unions, still with lustful and cruel rites, blood-revenge, and multiplied abominations ; wars and exterminations have their place ; everything objected to in the Old Testament, in short, reappears as part of the necessary development.

Is the case much mended ? How is the responsibility to be lifted from the God of Jesus into whose plan all this enters ? How are the difficulties—the contradictions—to be got over ? Is the problem not rather a hundredfold intensified ? For everything, immoral as it is, is now stamped with the print of Necessity, and made to be of divine origin as it never was before. Is the God who leads his moral creatures upwards through all this welter of evil, 'in accordance with the terrible law of the struggle of existence,' one whit easier to accept than the holy God of Abraham, Moses, and the prophets—even with His awful retributory judgments—in whom Jesus Himself believed ? Is a blind plunge into an abyss with a faith which involves a moral contradiction, a reasonable solution ? Why then is no element of faith in presence of an inscrutable Holiness, many of whose ways elude our judgment, permitted in the other case ? The question is one which, even from the 'modern' point of view, deserves consideration.

CHAPTER VI

THE ELEMENT OF MIRACLE IN REVELATION

It was seen at the commencement that it is deemed by many modern thinkers a sufficient reason for ruling out of consideration the question of supernatural revelation that it involves the element of *miracle*. In strictness, therefore, it might appear that the question of the *possibility* of special or supernatural revelation should have preceded the discussion of the *fact* of such revelation. On the other hand, if the *fact* is proved, this already disposes of many objections that may be taken to miracle on the grounds of abstract possibility or probability. The theoretic objection to miracle can have little force to minds already convinced of the existence and agency of a living, personal God, actuated by love to man, and desirous of bestowing on him the maximum of blessing. It was seen that it belongs to the very idea of God, in the full theistic view, to think of Him as self-revealing. And revelation is only complete when it becomes personal and special.

It is necessary now, however, that the miraculous element in revelation should be dealt with as a question by itself. General objections to miracle will be considered, but special attention will be given to the place and reasonableness of miracle as a factor in revelation.

I. Definition of Miracle.

1. For the sake of clearness, a distinction should be made between what may be called the *scientific* idea of miracle, and the *Biblical* or religious idea. In science, as in philosophy, miracle is defined with relation to the idea of *natural law*, or of a fixed order of nature, of which miracle then appears as an interruption. In the Biblical idea, a miracle is likewise an extraordinary event, evincing the immediate presence and operation of God, but it is measured rather by the *impression* it makes upon the mind, and by its *relation to the ends of revelation*, than by its relation to the natural order. It is an exaggeration, indeed, to say, as is sometimes done, that the Hebrews had no idea of an order in nature, and therefore felt no difficulty in conceiving of any number of miracles. There is no people on earth, beyond the most childlike stage, that has not some idea of the difference between ordinary and extraordinary events; and the Hebrews, with their faith in the creation and ordering of the world by God, had that idea in an unusually high degree. God had established the world by His word; had set bounds to sea and land by His decree; had ordained that seed-time and harvest, cold and heat, should not cease; had given measure and order to all things by His wisdom.[1] Still, it is the case that the idea of natural law, as now understood, was not possessed by the ancients, and that the Hebrews did not measure miracle by relation to this idea as moderns do. The essential thing in miracle was that there

[1] Cf. Gen. i. 14; viii. 22; Ps. xxxiii. 6-9; cxix. 90-1; Prov. viii. 29; Is. xl. 12, etc.

should be some plain and remarkable interposition of God for a holy end—say, for the help of His people, or the judgment of His enemies; and the question of *how* these extraordinary events were related to what we should call 'secondary causes,' or 'laws of nature' did not enter into consideration. Suppose it could be shown that any of these exceptional events, as, *e.g.*, the crossing of the Red Sea, were naturally mediated, this would not in the slightest degree alter its character as miracle in the Biblical sense of that word. The fact that it happened *then* and *there*, in connection with a revealed purpose, or by divine command, sufficed to guarantee its character as a divine interposition.

This Biblical idea of miracle is illustrated by the terms used to describe these extraordinary events in the Old and New Testaments. One class of terms brings out the *unusual*, exceptional, and striking character of the works (Heb. פֶּלֶא, נִפְלָאוֹת; Gr. τέρατα); another lays stress on the *power* displayed in them (Heb. גְּבוּרָה, גְּבוּרוֹת; Gr. δυνάμεις; a third gives prominence to their *teleological* significance—their character as 'signs' (Heb. אוֹת; Gr. σημεῖα). Alongside of these are terms which describe them simply as 'works' (Heb. מַעֲשִׂים or עֲלִילוֹת; Gr. ἔργα). It is the *purposeful* element which distinguishes the Biblical miracle from a mere portent or prodigy.

2. Miracle, in the *scientific* sense, as above remarked, is concerned with the relation to natural law. By miracle, in this connection, in distinction from the general idea of the supernatural, is to be

understood any real (not simply apparent) deviation from, or transcendence of, the ordinary course of nature, due to the interposition of a supernatural cause. The definition of miracle, with Hume and others, as a 'violation' of the laws of nature, is a question-begging and objectionable one. It suggests a sanctity belonging to the usual order of nature which is by no means to be attributed to it, and precludes the view that nature itself, in the divine purpose, may be subordinate to a higher spiritual order, whose ends call for an action of God above and beyond what nature is capable of. In nature itself one law crosses and modifies the action of another, and higher laws suspend or control the action of lower. Mechanical laws are over-ruled by chemical and vital. Gravitation is counteracted by the raising of the arm in obedience to an act of will. But nothing in nature is 'violated' thereby. The whole system of nature, in its reciprocal relations, is a unity, and all, in the last resort, depends on God, whose will, guided by His wisdom, is the ultimate law—the law of all laws, cause in all causes.

II. Possibility of Miracle.

1. It has just been observed that the abstract *possibility* of such divine interpositions as are alleged in miracle can scarcely be challenged by any one who admits the existence of the living, personal God. There are systems of the universe—atheistic, pantheistic, monistic, deistic—which, in their very nature, exclude miracle. Theism, if of a genuine and vital kind, as it is in the Christian

religion, creates even a presumption in its favour. For, as was formerly argued, a living, loving, personal God, can hardly do other than desire a more immediate fellowship with man than is provided for in the impersonal system of nature. Accordingly, in the region of the spirit—that with which revelation is chiefly concerned—large admissions are sometimes made by those who would dispute the occurrence of miracle in physical nature. Man's spirit is spoken of as open to immediate divine influences; God is described as entering into direct communion of spirit with man. 'How,' asks Dr. Martineau, in one place, 'should related spirits, joined by a common creative aim, intent on whatever things are pure and good, live in presence of each other, the one the bestower, the other the recipient of a sacred trust, and exchange no thought and give no sign of the love which subsists between them?'[1] Similarly Pfleiderer, 'Why should it be less possible for God to enter into a loving fellowship with us, than for men to do so with each other? I should be inclined to think that He is even more capable of doing so. For as no man can altogether read the soul of another, so no man can altogether live in the soul of another; hence all our human love is and remains imperfect. But if we are shut off from one another by the limits of individuality, in relation to God it is not so; to Him our hearts are as open as each man's heart is to himself; He sees through and through them, and He desires to live in them, and to fill them with His own energy and blessedness.'[2] But, if this be so, what becomes of

[1] *Study of Religion*, ii. p. 48.
[2] *Philosophy of Religion* (E.T.), iii. p. 305.

the argument against the possibility of supernatural revelation?

2. In Biblical revelation, however, miracle enters into the *physical*, as well as into the *spiritual*, sphere, and it is here that the objection to its admission is pressed at its keenest. 'The uniformity of nature,' as science has established it, is urged as an insuperable objection to the admission of physical miracle. The chain of causes and effects in the natural system cannot, it is alleged, at any point be broken. Even granting the abstract *possibility* of miracle, the difficulties of *proof* are held to be so great that no miracle, supposing one to happen, can ever be satisfactorily established by evidence. The preponderant presumption must always be against it. On the *historical* side, the evidence for miracle in the Bible is declared hopelessly to break down on critical examination. On this threefold ground of *possibility*, *credibility*, *historicity*, the miracles of Scripture are pronounced to be discredited. But this verdict may very reasonably be challenged.

III. Miracle and Law.

1. It must have been with some sense of the irony of his own argument that an acute reasoner like Hume laid down the position that 'a miracle is a violation of the laws of nature, and as a firm and unalterable experience has established these laws, the proof against a miracle, from the nature of the fact, is as entire as any argument from experience can possibly be imagined.' Again: 'It is a miracle that a dead man should come to life, because that has never been observed in any age or

country.'[1] It may be remarked in passing that, if the establishing of laws of nature depended, as Hume supposes, on proof of 'a firm and unalterable'—that is, a universal—'experience,' no law of nature could ever be made good. For such a universal induction is, in strictness, impossible. Laws of nature, in reality, are usually established by a comparatively *small* number of experiments, skilfully conducted, and verified by repetition. The (general) uniformity of nature is the postulate of, rather than the conclusion from, such experiments. But taking Hume's proposition as it stands, how glaring is the *petitio principii* involved in it! How is it made out that 'a firm and unalterable experience' has established that there are no exceptions to the ordinary course of nature? For this the proposition must mean if it is to have any validity as argument. Only by first ruling out all testimony to a contrary experience. A dead man cannot rise to life, *because* this has never been observed in any age or country. But has it not? This is the very thing to be proved. Hume *assumes* in his general proposition that no one has ever had experience of a miracle, then adduces this as *proof* that miracles have never happened!

2. Not a few in recent times endeavour to remove the difficulty attaching to the idea of miracle as contravention of nature by the hypothesis that miracles—the greatest included—are simply exceptions to what is *known* of the order of nature, and may be accounted for by the action of unknown powers or laws of nature.[2] There need be no hesita-

[1] *Essay on Miracles.*

[2] Cf. Dr. Sanday, *The Life of Christ in Recent Research*, ch. viii.

tion in admitting that much that belongs to the category of miracle in Scripture may possibly be thus explained. There is an 'economy' in miracle. Natural agencies are used as far as they will go.[1] But as a general theory of miracle this hypothesis labours under two obvious defects. (1) It can never be proved, and is in itself highly improbable, that the more signal exercises of miraculous power—*e.g.*, Christ's instantaneous cleansing of the leper, or raising of the dead, or His own resurrection—are simply adaptation of laws and forces already residing in nature; and (2) the theory does not dispense with a supernatural summoning into action and wielding of these hidden powers on a definite occasion and for a definite end. The miracle is not a spontaneous production of nature's laws; God's will is still involved in the wonder being wrought. A word is spoken, a command is given, God's interposition is invoked, and the marvel follows. It is in the *divine interposition*, whatever the mediate agencies employed, that the essence of the miracle lies.

IV. Credibility of Miracle.

1. A stronger position is taken up when objection is based, not on the general possibility of miracle, but on the *credibility* of the testimony by which the miracle is supported. It is unquestionable that, in the ordinary conduct of life, suspicion attaches to all narratives of supernatural, or even of very extraordinary, events. The presumption against a miracle is always strong; human testimony, where

[1] In the flood, the destruction of Sodom, the strong wind at the crossing of the Red Sea, etc.

marvels are concerned, is notoriously fallible. How then, Hume plausibly argues, can the one ever be successfully weighed against the other? Is it not always more likely, even where the witnesses are entirely honest, that a mistake has occurred, than that a real miracle has happened? As against this, it is to be remembered, generally, that the bulk of *all* our knowledge, ordinary and extraordinary alike, rests on testimony. It has often been pointed out that, with the exception of the fractional part of experience which belongs to ourselves, this is true even of Hume's 'firm and unalterable experience.' The experience of others is known to us only through testimony. 'Experience' and 'testimony,' therefore, cannot in this indiscriminating way be pitted against each other. There is a natural instinct leading us to believe in testimony, and, after all deductions, testimony is more often true than false. General distrust of testimony would bring human existence to an end.

2. Judgment, therefore, must be applied to the testimony to miracle, as to other things, and when this is done, and *a priori* assumptions are discarded, it becomes apparent that testimony to miracle may be, and in given circumstances is, perfectly admissible. To adduce as instances of miracle such absurdities as 'a pen turned into a pen-wiper,' [1] or a 'centaur trotting down the street,' [2] is to play with the subject. Miracles, every one feels, are not to be looked for in ordinary experience. The report, therefore, of a casual, unconnected wonder, as that a dead person had come to life in an adjoining town or parish, would be justly received

[1] Matthew Arnold. [2] Huxley.

with incredulity, or, if well attested, a natural explanation would be sought for it. Let, however, the question be put —Is a miracle equally incredible, if occurring as part of, or in connection with, a general scheme of divine revelation (itself supernatural in character), or for some solemn or important end of God's Kingdom, or in connection with persons well-accredited as bearers of a divine message to mankind ?—few persons, unwarped by philosophical theory, will feel that they are entitled to answer with the same confidence. They will decline to dogmatise, and will ask that the evidence be produced, and the case put before them in all its bearings.

This, it must be urged, is the only reasonable attitude to take up in relation to the miracles connected with divine revelation in the Bible. It is not enough to say with Hume that the presumption against a miracle must always be greater than the presumption in its favour. The circumstances must be looked at. It is conceivable that the circumstances may be such that there is not only no antecedent presumption against the miracle, but a strong presumption for it. Given, *e.g.*, such a Person as Jesus Christ by His whole manifestation shows Himself to be, and miracles, including that of His own resurrection from the dead, become not simply *credible*, but *natural*. It may be easier to believe that such an One rose from the dead, than that death continued to hold Him. Or given again a great scheme of divine revelation, extending through successive dispensations, it is not incredible that miracles should be employed at the founding of such dispensations, or at great crises in their course. Similarly with testimony. Everything here again depends on the *kind* of testimony, and on the circumstances in which it is delivered. Human testimony may be very faulty. But there are cases in which the testimony is of such a character, is given by such persons, under such conditions, with reference to such events, and in such a manner, that, accepting Hume's own canon, it would do more violence to reason to reject it than is involved in its acceptance.

Where these two things coincide: (1) where the presumption is, in the nature of the case, not against, but in favour of the miracle; and (2) where the testimony is reliable, and the matter plainly one on which the witnesses are competent to judge, the evidence even for miracle, instead of being weak, may be very strong indeed.

3. In dealing with the evidence for miracle, it is well not to allow the mind to be unduly biassed by the marshalling of instances to show how, with the progress of knowledge, belief in miracle is gradually being driven out of one department of inquiry after another, and the reign of law established. This is the favourite method, *e.g.*, of Lecky in his *Rationalism in Europe*. It is pointed out how the progress of science has banished belief in miracle in numberless regions where it once flourished; has purged out legend and fable from history; has destroyed belief in witchcraft, etc. Learned men, we are reminded, once believed in witchcraft. Its reality was held to be proved by solemn judicial investigations. But ask—*what* was proved? The fact that a man took ill, or a cow died, and that words were spoken, or a look given, with which the misfortune

was connected. That is not proof of miracle. What had to be proved was actual compact with, and the agency of, Satan, and that could only be done through extorted confessions, ordeals, and the like—a totally different case from the Biblical miracles. It is quite true that advance in enlightenment has banished a world of fables and superstitions from belief, and made the conditions of the proof of miracle more stringent. But is the effect necessarily to discredit *all* miracles, especially the class of miracles with which we have here to do ?[1] What if the effect of the scrutiny should only be to strengthen the evidence for the latter by bringing out on how completely different a footing they stand ? The same remark applies to the alleged 'ecclesiastical' miracles, in regard to which, to say the least, the greatest discrimination requires to be exercised.[2]

V. Historicity of Miracle.

1. Without dwelling longer on these abstract considerations, the real and practical question may now be looked at—How far the miracles which enter into the scheme of Biblical revelation are inherently credible and sufficiently attested. This is the question of *historicity*. It is not to be denied that the conditions of the discussion on this question are considerably altered from what they were in comparatively recent years. Take, *e.g.*, the old way of establishing the miracles of the period of the

[1] Butler's remarks on this point in his *Analogy*, Pt. II. ch. ii. and vii., well deserve consideration.

[2] Hume's test-case—the miracles at the tomb of the Abbé Paris—is dealt with, and effectually riddled, by Campbell in his *Dissertation on Miracles*. Cf. also Leland, *Deistical Writers*, Let. xix.

Exodus. First, the Pentateuch was shown by various lines of evidence to be the work of Moses; this was next held to give the narratives in Exodus the value of the testimony of an eye-witness; finally, it was shown that Moses did not deceive, and could not be deceived, in what he wrote. It would not be easy now to gain assent to the proposition that the Pentateuch, as it stands, is the work of Moses; so the argument breaks down at the outset. Similarly, the Gospels had first to be proved to be the genuine works of Matthew, Mark, Luke, and John; then the miracles were proved by the credit due to these witnesses. The intellectual outlook has changed, and, instead of basing belief in the revelation, as was formerly done, on the proof of the miracles, it is now customary to hold that it is the revelation that sustains credit in the miracles—so far as any credit is given to them. The miracles of Christ, *e.g.*, are believed in for Christ's sake; it is not the miracles that sustain faith in Christ.

There is undoubtedly a large element of truth in this position. It is freely granted that the miracles of Scripture cannot be satisfactorily proved as bare, external facts; they derive support from their place in, and connection with, the general scheme of revelation. On the other hand, it can in no way be conceded that historical evidence is no element in the proof. There *is* historical evidence, and that of a very cogent kind, for many of the greater miracles of Scripture—for the resurrection of Jesus Christ, for example. For others, the evidence is still considerable, and warrants a reasonable conviction of the truth of the event. Some miracles are entitled to our faith as belonging to groups or classes which may be regarded as strongly attested as a whole. We cannot, *e.g.*, prove independently each separate miracle of Jesus, but we may establish with great cogency that He *did* work miracles, and that miracles entered as a large element into the apostolic testimony about Him. Beyond this we are driven back on the internal character and general credibility of the narrative which records the miracle, on the connection of the miracles with the personalities by whom they were wrought, and the occasions on which they were wrought, and on the greater evidences which support the scheme of which they form a part as a supernatural system.

2. One error into which Hume and many since have fallen, is to assume that the only class of testimony available for miracle is *individual* testimony. It is the witness of the individual observer which alone is held to be of account. Then to this the most stringent tests are applied. This, however, unfairly represents the real strength of the case. It might be thought easier to prove an individual miracle than to establish the reality of a general supernatural system, of which the individual miracles form part. But it is not so actually. Just as Plato found it easier to study justice 'writ large' in the State before beginning to study it in the individual, so it will be found easier to establish the reality of a supernatural system on the large scale than to establish the special miracles which are, as it were, parts or corollaries of that system. The system, because it is taken as a whole, and regarded in its complete proportions, may be seen to exhibit evidences of supernatural origin which go far to sustain the credit of particular miracles associated with it.

Much of this evidence, internal to the system, has already been adverted to—the monotheism, *e.g.*, spirituality, organic unity, teleology, of the religion of the Old Testament; the unique doctrines and special adaptation to the needs of a sinful world of the Gospel of the New Testament; the element of prophecy, and fulfilment of the Old Testament in the New. These are proofs of the supernatural strain that runs through Scripture as a whole.

VI. Internal and External Evidence.

Hume, therefore, is wrong in staking everything on 'testimony,' and there solely on the witness of individual persons who can be cited and examined. The evidence for miracle is much wider in its scope.

1. It is not going too far to say that faith in miracle may rest on something other than external evidence of any kind. There is an *internal* evidence which often constrains faith where external evidence fails; which may be a substitute, or more than a substitute, for external evidence. 'Because thou hast seen Me,' said Jesus to Thomas, 'thou hast believed; blessed are they that have not seen and yet have believed.'[1] Suppose, for instance, that the Gospels had come into our hands without the least external clue to their authorship, origin, or the value to be attached to their testimony. Would it have been our duty to set them at once aside? Or would there not still have shone out from their narratives a convincing testimony to their essential truthfulness, and to the historicity of the divine portrait which they enshrine? The history contains

[1] See further in next chapter.

miracles. The account of these miracles interweaves itself with the whole narrative. They are congruous with the character of the Person who is the subject of the history. They are wrought, moreover, in connection with His work; are never mere *show* miracles. They have an ethical character and aim. They are not excrescences on the narrative, but are bound up with its substance, and associated with its profoundest and most original words. They are part of the material from which the picture of Jesus emerges. If He is historical, they are. Faith in them may be felt to be not only reasonable, but irresistible. Yet external evidence has not thus far been so much as touched on.

What applies to the Gospels in the New Testament applies also, though with necessary abatement of force, to many of the miracles of the Old Testament. We may not be able to connect the miracle in each case—or in any case—by a chain of evidence with the first witnesses. Yet we may have satisfying proof of a general scheme of revelation; we may have the presumption of miracle in that scheme, we may have the congruence of the miracle with its own stage of revelation, and with the actors in it; we may have the internal credibility of the narrative to which the record of the miracle belongs. We may have, as before, the ethical character and aim of the miracles; their interconnection with other elements of the history; their place as integral parts of a revelation confirmed by the subsequent history of the revelation. The revelation of God to Moses at the bush, for instance, is confirmed by the place which the revelation of God as Jehovah has in the after history of the people.

2. When transition is made from internal to *external* evidence, it does not follow that the latter—the external evidence—is to be narrowed down to the testimony of individual witnesses. Testimony may be *conjunct*, not individual; may be *national*, not personal; may be *in consciousness* and *experience*, not in documents merely; may be *monumental*, not in words. The testimony to the resurrection of Jesus, *e.g.*, is not weakened by the fact that it is the *conjoint testimony* of the whole body of the Apostolate—a testimony in which it never wavered or faltered. The entire New Testament rests on the basis of this harmonious apostolic testimony. Such events, again, as the Exodus of Israel, the crossing of the Red Sea, and the covenant at Sinai, rest not on the statements of the Book of Exodus only, but on the far broader basis of the unchanging *national consciousness* of Israel. The same is in a measure true of the facts of the patriarchal history, which the Exodus presupposes. The covenants with the fathers, and the promises made to them, are, as the Book of Deuteronomy shows, the bedrock of the people's consciousness of their relation to God.[1] Similarly, Christian experience—the *consciousness of the Christian Church*—needs such a history as that given in the Gospels to sustain it. The presence of the Holy Spirit in human hearts, in communities, in history, is as verifiable a fact as any we know. There is a Holy Spirit in the Church—the Fountain of light, of holiness, of power; the Source of sanctification, of renewal, of peace and joy. This effect—itself supernatural—needs a cause, and, tracing it back, the cause is only to be found in

[1] Cf. *Prob. of the O. T.*, pp. 93 ff. 100 ff.

that day when, the heavens being opened, Jesus, by the right hand of God exalted, poured forth that which men saw and heard.[1]

VII. Special Testimony to Miracles.

These considerations, it is granted, leave many questions open with regard to the *special miracles*. There may be no *a priori* objection to miracle as such; it may be allowed that miracle has a place in the scheme of revelation; but this still leaves undetermined the degree of evidence for this or that particular miracle. It has already been pointed out that the degree of this evidence greatly varies. For some miracles we have very strong evidence. Others belong to groups or classes strongly attested as a whole. For others the evidence is weaker, and we can only say of them that they are reasonable or credible in their general character, or in the place they hold in the system of revelation, or in connection with the general credibility of the account. Even on this subject, however, certain principles apply, which aid, to some extent, in judging of the miracles, even where they cannot be individually tested.

1. One such principle is the marked *reserve* and *discrimination* shown in the use of miracle in revelation. One frequently hears of the prodigality of miracles in Scripture. But this is a very erroneous impression, especially if comparison be made with other religions, where often the distinction of natural and supernatural is utterly abolished. What strikes

[1] Acts ii. 33. Examples of *institutional* testimony are seen in the Passover in the Old Testament, and the Lord's Supper and the observance of the Lord's Day in the New.

the careful reader of Scripture is rather what has been called the 'parsimony of miracles.' Miracle is not an element that runs through all Scripture equally, or appears with lavish prodigality anywhere. Miracles are, on the contrary, few, relatively to the length of the periods involved, and are distributed according to a wise and intelligible principle, viz.: that they are connected with the great epochs, and grouped around the great personalities in revelation. Apart from the theophanies, miracles hardly appear at all in Genesis. The only physical miracles, if such they can be called, are the flood and the destruction of the cities of the plain; both connected with natural causes. The period of the Exodus, and of the wilderness wanderings, is marked, as it was reasonable to expect, by great 'signs and wonders'—some score or more of miracles. The Conquest begins with a miracle—the fall of Jericho—after that no more.[1] Judges, apart again from the theophanies, is free from miracle, unless we reckon as such the signs of Gideon and the supernatural strength of Samson. The period of the kingdom is marked by hardly any miracles till the rise of the great prophetic figures, Elijah and Elisha, round whom miracles again cluster. The prophetic age is almost destitute of miracle. The dial of Ahaz and the fish of Jonah, with such a providential miracle as the destruction of Sennacherib's army, are nearly the only exceptions. The Book of Daniel has two miracles: the deliverance of the three Hebrews from the fire, and of Daniel from

[1] It is very doubtful if the standing still of the sun and moon in Josh. x. is not, as the quotation from the Book of Joshua suggests (ver. 12, 13), to be understood poetically.

the lions. From the close of Old Testament history after the exile till the time of Christ there are no recorded miracles. In the New Testament, there are the miracles of our Lord's infancy, ministry, and resurrection, and those connected with the founding of the Church by the apostles. John the Baptist wrought no miracles. Paul claimed the power of working miracles,[1] but history records few examples of its actual exercise. It will be difficult for any one to say that this is an extravagant profusion of miracles to be spread over the whole history of revelation.

2. Another principle, intimately connected with the foregoing, is that, as already remarked, the miracles of the Bible are never mere prodigies, or aimless displays of power, but stand in *close relation with the history of revelation*, and are strictly subordinate to its ends. They are wrought, not simply to strike wonder into the beholders, but for high and holy purposes, and to advance the ends of God's Kingdom. They are wrought mainly through the agency of, or in connection with, the great *personages* of revelation, *e.g.*, Moses, Elijah, Christ, and are rendered credible by their connection with these persons, and by the marks of sobriety and truthfulness in the history generally. This unique character of the Biblical miracles appears pre-eminently in the miracles of Christ, but is not confined to these. The law may be said to be a general one.

3. For the rest, it may be affirmed that the testimony of the greater miracles of Scripture *does*, in one form or another, *go back to eye-witnesses*,

[1] Rom. xv. 18, 19.

though the process of the testimony cannot always be traced. The connection of Moses with the books that bear his name may be left to criticism to determine. The credibility of the books is not destroyed by any difficulties about authorship. The miracles of the Mosaic period, if real, were wrought on a vast and imposing scale, and were witnessed by a whole generation of Israelites. Could the essential facts ever be forgotten? The vividness and dramatic character of the narratives seem to attest that records must have come down from a time not far removed from the events; that, at least, the narratives took shape when tradition was still fresh and reliable. The histories of Elijah and Elisha plainly come from the schools of the disciples of these prophets, and the strain of miracle in the narratives might be set down to the later glorification of legend, were it not that it is found in these prophetic histories *alone*, is congruous with the personages concerned, and with the crisis of the age in which they lived, and is so deeply embedded in the narratives that it is hardly possible to eliminate it without destroying the whole story. The characters of the prophets themselves have a life-like forcefulness which speaks to the truth of the portrayal. The narratives of Christ's miracles in the Gospels rest on a firm foundation of apostolic testimony. They place us throughout in contact with original witness. Matthew, who contributes at least the groundwork of the narrative that bears his name, was an eye-witness. John was an eye-witness. Mark was the companion and 'interpreter' of Peter. Luke put in writing those things which had been delivered by 'eye-witnesses and ministers of the word.'[1] The whole tradition of the life of Jesus must have been wrought into shape, and fixed in the form in which it comes to us in the Synoptics, during the years of the close association and preaching of the apostles at Jerusalem. The product in the Gospels is 'worthy of all acceptation.'

[1] Luke i. 1, 2.

CHAPTER VII

JESUS CHRIST—THE SUPREME REVEALER AND SUPREME MIRACLE

DISCUSSION returns at length to the Personality in whom all revelation is summed up—the One towards whose advent in the fulness of the times [1] all the lines of God's providence converged; whose appearance, when He did come, formed the starting-point for the world's future. Jesus is, without exaggeration, at the present moment, the centre of the interest of the world. He is 'set for the falling and rising again of many.' [2] Thoughtful minds feel that the task is laid upon them of explaining Him; of coming to some understanding with Him. The heathen peoples—rival systems of religion, in India, China, Japan, elsewhere—are awakening to realise that it is with Jesus and His religion they have to do; that the supreme question for their future is the acceptance or rejection of His claims.

I. 'MODERN' VIEW OF JESUS.

To those who deny supernatural revelation Jesus is necessarily a *problem*. What are they to make of Him? The one thing they are sure of is, that the supernatural claims set up for Him cannot be admitted. Whatever their admiration for His Person-

[1] Gal. iv. 4.

[2] Luke ii. 34.

ality and religion, He must be brought and kept within purely human limits. To show how this may be successfully done is the aim of numerous recent efforts at depicting His life and work. There are many schools in the negative camp, but this is the common denominator of them all—the gravitation-level to which they all tend. Jesus must be non-miraculous.

1. The Jesus of the new 'modern' school *is represented thus.* The ground fact is that a young Galilean peasant, son of Joseph and Mary of Nazareth, starting as a disciple of John the Baptist, became, about his thirtieth year, the originator of a remarkable religious movement in Galilee. This brought Him into collision with the Pharisees and ecclesiastical heads of the nation, and led, after perhaps a year's activity, to His being arrested at Jerusalem at the Passover, and, after trial by the Sanhedrim, and before Pontius Pilate, put to death by crucifixion as a blasphemer. Whether, as the Gospels say, He claimed for Himself the title Messiah is a moot question; whether He spoke the Apocalyptic discourses attributed to Him is held to be even more doubtful. Probably, as most allow, He did both, and to that extent, as in many other particulars of His thinking, was a victim of delusion, or shared the erroneous beliefs of His age. But His soul was one of singular purity—not 'sinless,' for the modern mind dare not use so absolute a word; His religious and ethical ideals were the most spiritual yet given to mankind; while the filial confidence He exercised in the Father, His perfect love and sympathy with men, and the continual polemic which cost Him His life against the merely

outward, ceremonial, and legal in religion, in favour of a spiritual worship, and an inward morality of the heart, made Him, in another sense than the theological, the true Founder of a Kingdom of God on earth. He gave up His life on the Cross in fidelity to His convictions, but, it need not be said, according to this new reading, did not rise again. It is allowed that His disciples believed He did, and even that they had seen Him, and that it was by the energetic preaching of a Risen Lord that the Christian Church was founded. These dreams, however, we are told, are gone, and the Church of the future will have to content itself with a Jesus on whose grave, as Matthew Arnold said, the Syrian stars still look down.

2. Such is the picture. What is to be said of it? What can be said of it, except that, professing to be 'religious-historical,' it is *not* historical in any real sense of the word? It is a picture to be rejected, not on any *a priori* dogmatic grounds, but simply because it does not fit the facts. It does not explain the Jesus of the Gospels. It does not explain the faith and hope of the early Christian Church, based on the facts which the Gospels record. It does not explain the vast effects which have come from the appearance and work of this Jesus. It does not explain how even such an image of Jesus came to be there—who created it, or could create it, or whence the materials came from which it was composed. It does not explain the edifice of Christian life, work, hope, and aspiration which has been built on Jesus, and, despite of all assaults on it, has endured through the ages. It does not explain Christian experience, Christian character, Christian enthu-

siasm and enterprise, the consciousness of redemption through Christ which lies at the foundation of all.

II. The Self-Consciousness of Jesus.

Instead of taking this picture critically to pieces, as has so often been done, the more positive task may be attempted of regarding Jesus in the light of His own revelation of Himself and of the Father. In this may be found the most effective refutation of the opposite representation.

1. The study of Jesus begins with His own consciousness of Himself—with His *self-consciousness* in its essential contents. The central point in Christ's self-consciousness is usually sought in His *filial spirit*—in his sense of *Sonship* to God. He felt and knew Himself from the beginning to be *a*, or more correctly *the*, Son of God. It is true that Jesus had this uninterrupted consciousness of Sonship; but it is an error to speak as if this consciousness explained itself, or was the most original element in His experience. It is customary to say that from Christ's consciousness of *Sonship*—from his possession of the filial spirit—was derived His conception of God as *Father*. But the knowledge of God as Father is not a deduction from Christ's consciousness of being a Son. It is the other way. It is through the knowledge of God as Father that the spirit of filial confidence, surrender, obedience, and love, is awakened. The two things grow up together, but of the two the intuition of God as Father necessarily takes the precedence. This again is given, not as a result of inference or reasoning, but as an original revelation in the soul of Jesus; a veritable intersphering of

the consciousness of the Father and the Son. 'I am in the Father, and the Father in Me.'[1] 'No one knoweth the Son, save the Father; neither doth any know the Father save the Son, and He to whomsoever the Son willeth to reveal Him.'[2] The fact of this immediate knowledge which Christ had of the Father may be psychologically inexplicable, but it is none the less real—a 'mystery of godliness.'[3]

2. With this original element in Christ's consciousness is to be taken a second: *His sinlessness.* This was Christ's own consciousness regarding Himself, and it was the unanimous belief and testimony of His followers about Him: He was without sin.[4] There is, quite naturally, something like a feeling of resentment growing up among the 'moderns' that 'sinlessness'—perfect holiness—unbroken harmony of mind and will with God—should be attributed to Jesus. Christ's own saying is often quoted as proof of the opposite: 'None is good save One, even God.'[5] But this is to mistake the meaning of the passage. Even in the case of Jesus there was a contrast between the ethical, developing goodness, advancing to its human perfection through trial and suffering, of which He was the subject—'Though he was a Son, yet learned He obedience by the things which he suffered'[6]—and the absolute, eternal goodness of the Godhead. The realised perfection of the Father was the archetype even for Him. This was a truth of which the rich young man, with his light use of the title 'good,' and his superficial ideals of goodness,

1 John xiv. 10. 2 Matt. xi. 27. 3 1 Tim. iii. 16.

4 2 Cor. v. 21; 1 Pet. ii. 22; 1 John iii. 5, etc.

5 Mark x. 18. Thus Schmiedel, Bousset, G. B. Foster, etc.

6 Heb. v. 8

needed to be reminded. But there is in this acknowledgment no confession or consciousness of personal sin on the part of Jesus. That was an element perfectly foreign to His mind. Jesus never once confesses sin, or prays for forgiveness of sin. With the purest and profoundest consciousness of what sin was in others, He betrays not the slightest trace of knowledge of sin in Himself; indeed, repels the imputation.[1] His mission in the world is to save sinners.[2] In the very fact of his taking such a *rôle*, He distinguishes Himself *from* sinners.

The moral perfection ascribed to Jesus is not less evident from the actual survey of *His character*. As depicted in the Gospels, He is 'holy, guileless, undefiled, separated from sinners.'[3] One is struck by the unexampled way in which the greatest ethical contrasts meet in the perfection of Jesus. With the most wonderful universality of nature is seen combined the keenest individual sympathy; with marvellous majesty, the greatest meekness and lowliness of heart; with unsullied purity, the tenderest solicitude for the recovery of the fallen. Dignity in this character is joined with repose; the loftiest claims with the gentlest condescension; intensest devotion with constant practical activity; burning zeal for holiness with an all-compassionating mercy. Wondrous wisdom is combined with yet more wondrous patience towards those who are slow of understanding and heart. The will of this holy being never swerves from God's will. God's end is His end; He so embodies and incarnates God that

[1] John viii. 46; xiv. 30.
[2] Matt. i. 21; ix. 19, 20; Luke, xix. 10.
[3] Heb. vii. 26.

He can say: 'He that hath seen Me hath seen the Father.'[1]

3. This consciousness of sinlessness in Jesus, coalescing with the consciousness of His unique relation to the Father, must, from the beginning, have made a *distinction between Him and others*, of which He could not but have been aware. Such a consciousness, moreover, could not have been present without awakening in Him the sense of a *vocation*. He alone knew the Father. He knew Himself to be separated from others by His freedom from sin, at the same time that He felt Himself knit to them by bonds of tenderest love. From these roots developed the consciousness that He was 'sent,' with a mission peculiar to Himself, to save and bless the world. This sense of vocation is an element in Christ's consciousness equally original with the others. It was there in germ from the first.[2] It was part of the revelation of the Father in His soul. The mode and stages of this consciousness of vocation—what is named particularly *Messianic* consciousness—are necessarily obscure. But from the period of the Baptism it is manifest, and can be studied in its completed form. In this Messianic consciousness, Jesus connects Himself with the past. He knows Himself to be the goal and fulfilment of all Old Testament revelation. He fulfils law and prophets.[3] He appropriates to Himself all prophecies and promises relating to the Messiah.[4] He is the King—the Son of David—the

[1] John xiv. 9.

[2] It is manifest in His words when found in the temple with the doctors, Luke ii. 48-50.

[3] Matt. v. 17. [4] Mark ix. 12; Luke xxiv. 25-27.

Founder of the Kingdom of God and Lord over it. Even while spiritualising the idea of the Kingdom, and freeing it from all national and legal limitations, He holds fast to the essential prophetic conception of a future realised reign of righteousness among men.[1] He knows what is written of the superhuman dignity, exalted prerogatives, and future triumphs of the coming King.[2] He identifies Himself with Isaiah's 'Servant of Jehovah'[3]—specially with what is foretold of the Servant's humiliation and atoning suffering, and of His after victory.[4] He connects His death with the redeeming sacrifice of the Passover.[5] His Messianic vocation meant *salvation* to the world. It meant sacrifice, consecration, surrender of His life for others, a death which was *redemption*.[6] His consecration at the Baptism meant the acceptance of this vocation. Jesus saw from that first hour what lay before Him; knew that He must die. The second and third temptations show His definite choice of the path of the Cross in opposition to false and worldly ideals of Messiahship.[7]

4. Yet another element in this original consciousness of Jesus is the consciousness of *supernatural powers*. This is with Him at least from the time of the Baptism—probably earlier. In the perfect purity of His nature, and unbroken consciousness of Sonship with God, He stood in unique *rapport* also with the forces of the natural and spiritual worlds. These were at His disposal.[8] Miraculous power is implied in the first temptation, while in this temptation there is the renunciation of all use

[1] Matt. vi. 10. [2] Cf. Is. ix. 6, 7. [3] Luke iv. 21.
[4] Luke xxii. 37. [5] In the Lord's Supper.
[6] Matt. x. 28. [7] Cf. Matt. iv. 5-11. [8] Matt. viii. 7-13.

of this power for His own personal ends.[1] The miracles of Jesus—supernatural to us—were natural to Him; were, as John calls them, His 'works.'[2]

5. From the depths of the unique consciousness of Jesus sprang naturally His *claims*. These claims, stupendous and arrogant, if judged by a merely human standard, are but the expression of His knowledge of Himself, of His mission, of His divine authority, of the work the Father had given Him to do. He knew whence He was, and whither He went; hence He alone could adequately testify of Himself.[3] He was 'Son of Man,' but also 'Son of God'—both expressions being used in a unique and pregnant sense. He had divine authority to forgive sins. He had all authority given to Him in heaven and in earth.[4] He baptized with the Holy Spirit. He was Fulfiller of the Old Testament; Messiah; King; Lord of men. He was the Saviour of the world; was likewise the Judge of the world. By relation to Him the everlasting destinies of men were determined.[5] There is no need to imagine 'little Apocalypses'[6] to account for the eschatological sayings of Jesus. The eschatological utterances came from the same self-consciousness as the rest of His claims. After He had died, He predicted, He would rise again.[7] He would return in the glory of His Father, and with the holy angels.[8] Exalted to heaven, He would send the Spirit, and be with His disciples till the end of the world.[9]

[1] Matt. iv. 3, 4.
[2] *E.g.*, John v. 36; x. 25, 32, 38, etc.
[3] John viii. 14.
[4] Matt. xi. 27; xxviii. 18.
[5] Matt. xxv. 31-46.
[6] Thus modern critics.
[7] Matt. xvi. 21, etc.
[8] Matt. xiv. 27; xxv. 31, etc.
[9] Matt. xxviii. 20; Luke xxiv. 49; John xv. 26, etc.

III. Supernatural Estimate of Jesus.

How are such a life, such a Personality, such a consciousness, such claims, to be explained? Out of mere humanity? Out of evolution? Then must Jesus have been like other men; of finer, grander genius, perhaps, but essentially of the same mould as they, with frailty, imperfection, sin, adhering to Him. But this, we have just seen, He was not. How then explain Him? How did such a life begin? For such an One as Jesus actually was a unique origin must be postulated; such a *superhuman* beginning as the first and third Gospels narrate. How did such a life end? In death? Or in triumph over death: in conquest of death: in *resurrection*, as the Gospels again assert? In affirming the Virgin Birth and the Resurrection of Christ, we affirm only that the life of Christ is of a piece; that it is congruous with itself, and with the claims which Christ made throughout His whole life.[1]

Jesus rose from the dead. His resurrection is the pre-eminent miracle of the New Testament; the miracle which guarantees many others, and sets the seal of truth on the claims to Messiahship and divine Sonship that went before.[2] It was the rock on which the apostolic Church was founded; and unbelief has not yet succeeded in removing that rock from its place. Rather does the fact become surer with the failure of every new attempt to explain it away. Imposture is given up by all intelligent minds; the theory of swoon—of *apparent* death—was shattered

[1] The author has discussed the Virgin Birth of Christ and the Resurrection in works bearing these titles. [2] Rom. i. 4.

beyond recall by the criticism and irony of Strauss; changes have been rung on the *vision*-theory till men in utter weariness are deserting it, and falling back on the view of 'apparitions' of the dead Jesus; that hypothesis, again, is giving place to theories of derivation of the belief from Babylonian, Persian, and other pagan myths. Meanwhile, 'the firm foundation of God standeth,' [1] and Easter hymns are sung as of old in all lands from the sun's rising to its setting!

The resurrection and exaltation of Jesus shed light back upon His claims while He was on earth—interpret them, complete them; but, further, His exaltation shows the ultimate ground of these claims in the *full divine dignity* of His Person. He who is raised to the throne of divine dominion; who is worshipped with honours due to God only; [2] who is joined with Father and with Holy Spirit as, co-ordinately, the source of grace and blessing,[3] *must* in nature be divine. There is not such a thing as honorary Godhead. Hence the apostolic doctrine of Christ's Person, 'The Word was God. . . . The Word became flesh. . . . The only-begotten Son who is in the bosom of the Father, He hath declared Him.' [4] Hence, as an immediate corollary, the absoluteness of Christ's *revelation*. Jesus is the Supreme Revealer, not simply by what He said, but by what He was, by what He did, and by what He *now is*. No other can succeed Him, or displace Him, or supersede His revelation. 'In whom are

[1] 2 Tim. ii. 19.
[2] John v. 23; Phil. ii. 9-11; Rev. v. 8-14, etc.
[3] 2 Cor. xiii. 14; Rom. i. 7, etc.
[4] John i. 1, 14, 18; cf. Phil. ii. 6-11.

all the treasures of wisdom and knowledge hidden.'[1] All-embracing in its scope, universal as the needs of humanity, His revelation is yet germinal in its fulness, embodying ideas, laws, principles, which, under the guidance of the Spirit, it lies with future ages to unfold.

IV. Aspects of Christ's Revelation.

1. It has been made a reproach to the religion and morality of Jesus that He did not busy Himself with the *secular* or *mundane* side of life—with education, with art, with economics, with politics. Strauss, J. S. Mill, Mazzini,[2] and others more extreme, have made this objection to Jesus. But there lies in such a charge a grave misapprehension of the nature of Christ's revelation. Jesus did not busy Himself with these secular interests; not, however, because He despised these things, for, as His parables abundantly show, they were parts of a divine order which He fully recognised. The world to Him, with all its fulness of social relations and interests, was God's world; a world which it was His to redeem, and bring into harmony with the will of God. If Jesus did not busy Himself directly with these things, it is because He did better. Had Jesus intermeddled with the social order of His time; had He laid down rules for the regulation of capital and labour, of rulers and subjects, of bond and free; had He spent His brief ministry in discussing art, or education, or politics, His teachings long ere this would, like those of other teachers, have become obsolete.

[1] Col. ii. 3, 9.
[2] Mill in essay on *Liberty*; Mazzini in *Essays*, v. p. 363.

The order of the world changes, and rules applicable to one age or stage of society would not be applicable to another. Hence Christ disclaimed such interference. 'Man, who made me a judge or a divider over you?'[1] He had higher work to do. But *this* He did; He gave to the world the great regulative ideas in which lie the solution of all these problems. He enunciated great principles, gave great master-truths which are to be the light of our seeing in all our discussions of such questions, and of our legislation upon them. He did not, *e.g.*, enter on a crusade against slavery, which in that age would have been futile. But He laid down principles as to the nature of man and man's relation to God—as to the infinite value of the soul and the essential equality of all men before God—which struck at the very foundations of slavery, and were bound eventually to abolish it, as they have done in all Christian lands.

2. This, however, was not the highest or peculiar sphere of Christ's revelation. To reach the kernel of that, it is necessary to go back to His own chosen expression for the message He brought; '*the Kingdom of God*.' The Kingdom of God was the subject which continually filled Christ's thoughts. It defined for Him the end of God's purpose in the world, and therefore of His own mission. The Kingdom of God is a conception of many sides and aspects. Yet, as Jesus apprehended it, the core of the idea is simple. It is simply the expression for a *reign of God in humanity*—for the supremacy of God, or of God's will, in human hearts and human affairs, and in every department of these affairs. 'Thy Kingdom come. Thy will be done, as in heaven, so on

[1] Luke xii. 14.

earth.'[1] The Kingdom of God begins *within*, in the new life imparted to the soul by Christ, but the Kingdom is not intended to *remain* within. It is to work itself out into all the spheres and relations of our human life, and God's will is to be made supreme in each. It is to work itself out into the family, and God's will is to be made supreme there; into social relations, business relations, civic relations, political relations; into arts, commerce, literature, amusements; and God's will is to be made supreme in all. There could not be a principle more practical or comprehensive.

3. In Christ's doctrine of the Kingdom of God are embodied all *the great truths* of His revelation. Here most clearly it is seen that the truth He reveals is of a kind that, in the nature of the case, can never become obsolete. His words cannot pass away.[2] The revelation flows from Himself—from the depths of His personal consciousness—and is therefore inseparable from Himself.

(1) Jesus teaches, first, of *God His Father*, and truth about God, His being, His character, His purposes, His love and forgiving grace, if only it *be* truth, is truth eternal as God Himself.

(2) Jesus teaches about *man*, but about man in what relations? Not from the point of view of rank, or age, or race, or sex, or culture; but from the point of view, solely, of man as a spiritual and immortal being, in His relations to God and to eternity. In this light alone Christ regards man, speaks of man, legislates for man, calls man to Himself. He is tenderly sympathetic, indeed, to man in his weaknesses and afflictions. He comes eating and drinking.

[1] Matt. vi. 10. [2] Matt. xxiv. 35.

He sits at the marriage feast. He keenly observes the varied play of life around Him. But it is man, the spiritual being, He is ever beholding in, and through, and behind all this. Jesus deals with the universal, the abiding, the essential, in man. It is this which gives His words weight, and makes them enduring. They are words for all ages and stages of civilisation; for all grades of culture; for highest and lowest races; for all conditions of human life. Himself the embodiment of God's ideal of man ('Son of man'), as, on the other side, He is the ideal embodiment of God to man ('Son of God'), He reveals man to himself and in his relations to the Father. As correlative to His doctrine of God's *Fatherhood*, He awakens in man the consciousness of *brotherhood*.

(3) Jesus teaches, again, about *sin*—another universal fact in humanity. Sin is that which involves humanity in spiritual ruin, frustrates man's true destiny to a life of sonship in God's Kingdom, and creates the need of redemption. Himself pure in every thought and act, Jesus speaks of sin as a power in the heart as well as a fact in the outward life,[1] describes it as bondage and disease, as entailing guilt and, in its awful issues, doom,[2] and as imperatively calling for divine deliverance. He reveals *grace* and *forgiveness*, and connects salvation with His own Person and work, peculiarly with His death.[3] He calls sinners to repentance.

(4) Jesus teaches about *righteousness*: the righteousness of the Kingdom; and, in opposition to Phari-

[1] Matt. xv. 19; John iii. 3 ff. etc.

[2] Matt. vii. 23; Luke xiii. 3, 5; John viii. 24, etc.

[3] Matt. xx. 18, 19, 28; John iii. 14, 15; vi. 51; x. 15, etc.

saic literalism, formalism, and hypocrisy, expounds that righteousness as flowing from its two principles of love to God and love to man.[1] His ideals are not the world's. In most respects they are the inversion of the world's ideals, involving, to borrow a phrase from Nietzsche, the least sympathetic of men with Christ's religion, a 'transvaluation of all values.' They directly invert ordinary human standards, in everything subordinating the material to the spiritual, the temporal to the eternal, the goods of the body to the goods of the soul.

(5) Lastly, Jesus teaches about *salvation*, or, as it is often phrased, 'eternal life.' This is the ultimate blessing of God's Kingdom—participation in God's own holy, blessed, incorruptible life, a life which in its nature is above change and death, which, beginning here, is nourished by the knowledge of God and fellowship with Him,[2] and culminates in the immediate vision of God in eternity.[3]

The very enunciation of such truths proclaims the absoluteness and enduringness of Christ's revelation. A Kingdom of God based on such truths cannot be *only* of earth ; it points beyond, and can only attain its consummation in the eternal world.[4] Immortality —'incorruption'—perfecting in holiness—complete redemption from sin, pain, and death—union with all the good—are involved in its very conception.

4. While Christ is the Revealer, His revelation is not to be divorced from, still less opposed to, *the apostolic Gospel*, which further unfolds its import.

[1] A chief exposition is in the Sermon on the Mount.
[2] John xvii. 3.
[3] John xvii. 24 ; 1 Cor. xiii. 12 ; Rev. xxii. 3, 4, etc.
[4] Matt. xiii. 43 ; xxv. 34 ; Rev. vii. 13-17, etc.

It was only in part that even Jesus could discover to His disciples the whole truth about Himself and His work; for salvation was to be through Himself, and His work had to be completed before it could be understood. The great sacrifice in which His mission on earth culminated had not yet been made, though it was looked forward to, and intimations were given of it.[1] The meaning of that sacrifice had afterwards to be unfolded. The *Cross* had to be shown to be the supreme revelation at once of the love and of the holiness of God. There sin and righteousness met together, the one to receive its decisive defeat through the other. Salvation from sin did not ignore law, or the law's condemnation of sin, but was accomplished through voluntary submission to the worst that sin could inflict, or that God's judgment on the sin of the world entailed.[2] Christ was obedient even unto the death of the Cross.[3] The completeness of His work, its acceptance by the Father, the finality of His conquest of sin and death, were attested by His resurrection in power, The apostolic Gospel but explains all this, and sets it in the full light shed on it by Christ's exaltation, and the mission of His Spirit.[4]

V. The Self-Humiliation of Jesus.

A question which necessarily arises out of the claim of Christ to be the medium of the absolute revelation of God to man—one which has been

1 Matt. xx. 28; xxvi. 28; John iii. 14-16; vi. 51, etc.
2 Rom. iii. 21-31; viii. 1-3; 2 Cor. v. 21, etc.
3 Phil. ii. 8.
4 John xiv. 25, 26; xv. 26, etc.

much discussed in recent times—relates to the *limitations of Christ's human consciousness.* It is the problem of the 'Kenosis,' or self-emptying of Christ in His incarnate life,[1] with its effects in limitation and possible error in His human knowledge. The question of the 'Kenosis' on its theological side, or as relates to the supra-temporal (divine) mode of Christ's being as Son, is here left out of view.[2] Even on the human side, however, it is to be noticed that the term 'Kenosis' has no appropriateness, save as the higher mode of being, and a voluntary condescension to the human state, are implied. On a humanitarian theory there may be limitation, but there can be no voluntary self-limitation, such as the Pauline term connotes. It may be desirable, therefore, to drop the use of this particular term, and speak simply of the limitations which belonged to Christ as man, and of the bearings of these on His revelation.

1. The tendency in recent discussion, it must have been observed, has been to push this doctrine of limitation very far. Even among those who accept the reality of the incarnation, and acknowledge Christ as, in His eternal being, 'very God of very God,' the disposition is to view Him in the incarnate state as so 'depotentiated' of all the attributes of Godhead as to be hardly distinguishable, in the growth and development of His human consciousness, from an ordinary man. He was not only humanly ignorant of all that did not belong to His direct mission, but was in actual error on many points.

[1] The term is derived from Phil. ii. 7: 'emptied Himself.'

[2] This aspect of the subject may be studied in Prof. A. B. Bruce's *Humiliation of Christ.*

He shared the views of his contemporaries, *e.g.*, on such matters as angels and demons, on the Old Testament Scriptures, on all matters of natural knowledge. To the 'modern' theologian, who rejects the supernatural side of Christ's Person altogether, such a conception presents no difficulties. Jesus, as man, naturally was a child of His age, and shared its errors. On either of these views, the absoluteness of Christ's revelation seems imperilled. If error inhered in Christ's thoughts of God, man, the world, sin, the Scriptures, spiritual existence, the future,—if His conceptions on these subjects were *naïve*, illusory, cast in the childlike and imperfect moulds which an unscientific age afforded,—what normative value can be ascribed to them? They may be beautiful, but are they true? Must not modern science and philosophy be called in to expurgate them, and tell us what 'kernel' of truth abides as the result? This is an attitude with which the foregoing representations are plainly incompatible.

2. On this subject the following remarks may be offered:—

(1) That Christ's human knowledge had its limitations is a necessary corollary from His assumption of a *true and real humanity*. This must be conceded, if the reality of the incarnation is to be maintained. As a babe in Bethlehem Jesus began His earthly existence without knowledge of any kind. In childhood and youth, He grew in wisdom as in stature.[1] He made no claim to omniscience as man. He asked questions which implied lack of information. He expressly disclaimed knowledge of the

[1] Luke ii. 40, 52. Cf. Calvin, *in loc.*

day and hour of His final advent.[1] No one who thinks seriously on the subject will maintain that, during His earthly life, Jesus carried in His consciousness a knowledge of all events of history, past, present, and future, of all arts and sciences, including the results of our modern astronomies, geologies, biologies, mathematics, of all languages, etc. To suppose this would be to annul the reality of His human consciousness entirely. The incarnation means that Jesus, in becoming man, entered into all the conditions of a true human life, growth and development included. If it be said that the knowledge was still there in Christ's omniscience as God, and that, had He *willed* to know, He would have known; that it was by voluntary act He did not know; it must still be granted that, as in the deliberate refusal to use His miraculous powers for personal ends, so in respect of any knowledge He might have possessed beyond what the Father gave Him, it was His will *not to know*. The limitations of His human consciousness were not assumed, but real.

(2) Does this acknowledged limitation of the human knowledge of Christ, and ignorance of earthly science, imply *error* on the part of Jesus? This is a position which must as strongly be contested. Ignorance is not error, nor does the one thing necessarily imply the other. That Jesus should use the language of His time on things indifferent, where no judgment or pronouncement of His own was involved, is readily understood; that He should be the victim of illusion, or false judgment, on any subject on which He was called to pronounce, is a

[1] Mark xiii. 32.

perilous assertion. If the matter be carefully considered, it may be felt that even sinlessness is hardly compatible with liability of the judgment to error. False judgment, where moral questions are involved, can hardly fail to issue in wrong action. Saul of Tarsus was sincerely persuaded that Jesus was a blasphemer, and counted that he was doing God service in persecuting His followers.[1] Suppose Jesus similarly to have erred in His judgment, in regard, say, to the Pharisees, and to have included in His sweeping condemnations a class which had in it many excellent, if somewhat misguided individuals, would this have involved no moral blame? This raises the vital question—Could Christ, as man, be preserved infallibly from error? The affirmative answer can only be given, if it is upheld that, in dealing with Jesus, we are truly dealing, not with an ordinary, but with a supernatural Person. Christ's was a true manhood, yet it was the manhood of One the root of whose being was in eternity. We are becoming accustomed to the idea of 'subliminal consciousness'—of a depth in personality from which issue impulses, monitions, intuitions, of which ordinary consciousness can give no explanation. *The subliminal consciousness in Jesus was Godhead itself.* From it came that fulness of knowledge and certainty regarding Himself, the Father and the Father's will, His mission and work in the world, which constituted His peculiar revelation. Is it too much to believe that there came from it also—what was equally essential for His vocation—those regulative influences and that subtle sensitiveness to truth and error, which issued,

[1] Acts xxvi. 8-11; cf. John xvi. 2.

when judgment had to be given, in sure and unerring insight?

3. Two crucial cases may be taken as instances. (1) The one is Christ's attitude to *the unseen spiritual world.* Jesus believed in angels, in Satan, in the reality of demoniacal influences. Was this, as is commonly assumed, illusion, or simple accommodation to prevalent belief? There is the strongest ground for thinking it was neither. That Jesus used popular and figurative language in speaking of these things proves nothing against the reality of the fact. If language has meaning, He unquestionably believed in a spiritual kingdom of evil whose power it was His mission to overthrow, and whose agency He recognised in the unhappy subjects of 'possession.'[1] Surely also if there is any one thing in which Christ's intuition can be trusted, it is in a matter of this kind, which turns on *rapport* with the spiritual world. That world, it can be confidently said, lay open to Him as it did to no other. What He solemnly affirmed of it could not be less than truth. The modern world may refuse to believe in anything it cannot bring to scientific tests, and explain by natural—in this case by psychological—causes. But there may be things in heaven and in earth which are above even the modern world's philosophy, and its eyes are perhaps opening a little to discern that this may be one of them.

(2) The other case is Christ's attitude to *the Scriptures.* Are His statements and declarations here

[1] It is not the case that all maladies are attributed to evil agency. Distinction is made between ordinary sickness, disease, and even lunacy, and possession (Matt. iv. 23, 24, ix. 32-5, x. 8, etc.)

to be taken as authoritative? What if modern criticism can show that many of them are wrong? Is the matter to be dismissed by saying that it was not Christ's mission to teach regarding such things? Or that He simply adopted the current erroneous views of His age? Here it may readily be admitted that when Jesus used popular language about 'Moses' or 'Isaiah,' He did nothing more than designate certain books, and need not be understood as giving *ex cathedra* judgments on the intricate critical questions which the contents of these books raise. Had such questions been proposed to Him for decision, He would probably have dealt with them as He did with the appeal about inheritance: 'Man, who made Me a judge or a divider over you?'[1] But Jesus unquestionably did believe in the Old Testament as the inspired record of God's revelations in the past,—did believe in the essential historicity of its contents,—did believe in Moses and his writings,—did believe in the law,—did believe that psalms and prophets pointed forward with unerring finger to Himself.[2] Was it Jesus who was wrong in this? Or is it criticism, so far as criticism denies these things? Jesus certainly had no more knowledge of the methods and processes of modern criticism than He had of modern astronomy or geology. But this does not imply that He was mistaken in His judgment on the Scriptures. The error lies in supposing that the only way of being assured of the truth of the revelation of God in the Scriptures is by modern critical study. Jesus, through His possession in its fulness of the Spirit that wrought in that earlier revelation, went with

[1] Luke xii. 14. [2] Luke xvi. 31, John v. 45-7, etc.

unerring certainty to the very heart of it. He not only penetrated to its truth, but intuitively perceived the inner connection of truth and history. Essential truth to Jesus implied historical truth. The truths of God's revelation were not in the air They became the possession of mankind through *real* events and *real* acts of God. Revelation, in a word, was *historical.* Hence the confidence with which Jesus uses the Old Testament Scriptures, and continually appeals to them as the word of God. This, it is granted, does not settle purely literary questions. But many literary questions are settled in principle when the Scriptures are approached as Jesus approached them.

CHAPTER VIII

REVELATION AND ITS RECORD—INSPIRATION

THE proposition may be laid down, that, if a revelation has been given, it is natural and reasonable to expect that a record will be made or kept of the stages of that revelation, either by its immediate recipients, or by those who stand within the circle of the revelation, and are possessed in an eminent degree of its Spirit. While the necessity of such a record, if revelation is not altogether to fail of its object, cannot of itself prove the existence of a code of sacred writings, it creates a presumption of their existence, and powerfully supports the claim of a body of Scriptures professing to satisfy this requirement, and actually presenting qualities answering to their claim.

I. PRELIMINARY POSITIONS.

A first point in the above proposition is, that, if a revelation has been given by God, it is reasonable to expect that provision will be made for *the preservation* of the knowledge of the revelation *in some permanent and authoritative form.* Otherwise the object in giving the revelation would be frustrated. The means of the transmission of knowledge may be oral, so long as oral tradition, combined with careful instruction,[1] can be depended on; or

[1] Exod. xii. 26, 27; Deut. vi. 7, 20 ff., lxxviii. 3, 4; Luke i. 1, 2, etc.; Gen. xviii. 19.

it may be partly oral and partly documentary; or it may be documentary from the beginning. It may not be possible now to trace all the links in this process of transmission; but the product may bear in itself evidence that the result intended has been surely accomplished.

Other points assumed in this proposition are that the record of His revelation which God gives will be made either (1) by the *original recipients* of the revelations (*e.g.*, the prophets wrote their own books, Paul his own Epistles, John his own Gospel); or (2) by those who *stand within the circle* of the *revelation* (*e.g.*, Mark and Luke belonged to the immediate apostolic circle); and (3) that those who produce the record *possess in an eminent degree the Spirit of the revelation*, and are fitted by insight and sympathy to produce the kind of record that is required for the purposes in view.

A yet more fundamental assumption underlying the proposition is, that there is, and has been from the beginning, *a Holy Spirit* in the community of believers who can and does confer these qualifications. The denial of the Holy Spirit in the community of God's people may fitly be described as *the primal heresy*—the heresy of all heresies—in the Christian Church. Scripture assumes as axiomatic a presence and work of the Spirit from its first page to its last.

II. Extension of the Idea of Revelation.

When the question is raised of the relation of revelation to its record, it is first to be noted that *an important extension* must be made of the idea of revelation—an extension carrying us much beyond the scope of the previous discussion. This in several respects.

1. It is obvious that the word must here be taken as including, not only direct divine acts and communications, but *the whole divinely-guided history* of the people of Israel, and, in the New Testament, *the apostolic action* in the founding of the Church. Here again the principle of the co-operation of divine providence with revelation for the subserving of the ends of the latter finds application.[1] To providence must be entrusted the securing and preserving of such materials as are necessary for a proper presentation of the history. These materials need not be the work of inspired men, but may come through the ordinary channels of information—may consist of traditions, monuments, state records, genealogies, etc., as well as written narratives. Inspiration is seen in the use made of these materials, not in the providing of them.

2. A further step is taken when it is observed that revelation ('unveiling'), in this wider sense, must be held to include the *insight* given by the divine Spirit into the *meaning* of the history, through which holy men are enabled to write it for the instruction of all ages.[2] It is analogous to, though, as befitted their special task, a higher degree of, that 'Spirit of wisdom and revelation' in the knowledge of Christ which is bestowed on all Christians[3]—a form of the revelation of *illumination* applied to the laws and workings of God's providence in the accomplishing of the ends of His kingdom. The prophetic

[1] See above, p. 23.
[2] 1 Cor. x. 11; 2 Pet. i. 20-21.
[3] Eph. i. 17.

insight is of necessity much deeper than that of the ordinary believer, because it is *prophetic*—a special endowment of the Spirit of revelation for a special end.

3. It is, however, not simply the history of revelation on its *divine* side which is of spiritual interest, but the *human reception* also of that revelation, and the *actings of the human spirit* under its influence, and in response to it, which are to be taken into account. This also is a necessary part of the unfolding of the meaning of revelation. In other words, there is needed, in a book which is to be the record of divine revelation, not only the record of what may be called its *external* historical course, but the record of its *internal* history in the life and experience of souls that have grasped its meaning, and felt its power. What, for instance, would the record of revelation be in the Old Testament without the Book of Psalms ?

It begins to be evident that a record of revelation in the broad sense includes a great deal more than the divine acts and communication, or even the history, with which we began. It includes psalms, songs, wisdom-teaching, Epistles,—records of human doubt, struggle, temptation, victory, — sections which unfold the *principles* of revelation, apply and enforce them, turn them into subjects of praise, deal with them reflectively as doctrine. All this, too, in a very important sense, is revelation. A very weighty conclusion follows. We began rightly by distinguishing between revelation and the record of revelation. There is an important truth in that distinction, for it marks the fact that there is an objective revelation in divine acts and words prior to any written record. But we have now found that the line between revelation and its record is becoming very thin, and that, in another true sense, *the record*, in the fulness of its contents, *is itself for us the revelation.* There are parts of the revelation—some of the prophetic discourses, *e.g.*, or the Epistles—which never existed in any but written form. But the record as a whole is the revelation—God's complete word—for us. Its sufficiency is implied in the fact that beyond it we do not need to travel to find *God's whole will* for our salvation.

III. Inspiration—the Biblical Conception.

We are thus brought to the particular consideration of the much-debated subject of *inspiration*—a subject in the treatment of which, all will allow, peculiar difficulties emerge.

Two methods present themselves in dealing with this subject.

1. We might analyse, as has often been done, the *testimony of Scripture* to its own inspiration, then proceed to inquire how far the facts agree with this testimony. Or—

2. We may begin with *the facts* which illustrate the *nature* of inspiration, as seen in the book itself, then endeavour to show how this agrees with the witness of Scripture to itself.

For the end at present in view the latter is the preferable course. It assumes nothing, and is not open to the objection of forcing the phenomena of Scripture into harmony with any preconceived theory. Still, some indication of the general view taken of inspiration by the Biblical writers cannot be wholly omitted. It may surprise those who have not looked into the subject with care to discover how strong, full, and pervasive, the testimony of Scripture to its own inspiration is. Meanwhile it may suffice to recall the summary which the apostle gives of the qualities imparted by inspiration to Scripture in what may be called the *classical* passage on the subject—that, viz., in 2 Tim. iii. 15-17.

Comparing this passage as it stands in the Authorised Version with the form it has in the Revised Version, it will be observed that certain important changes are made in the latter.

1. In verse 15, the words 'Holy Scriptures' are more correctly translated 'sacred writings.' The terms (*τὰ ἱερὰ γράμματα*) are different from those used in ver. 16, 'every Scripture' (*πᾶσα γραφή*) The verse then reads: 'That from a babe thou hast known the sacred writings which are able to make thee wise unto salvation through faith which is in Christ Jesus.'

2. Instead of the translation, 'All Scripture is given by inspiration of God, and is profitable,' etc. the alternative rendering is preferred: 'Every Scripture inspired of God is also profitable,' etc. The R. V. margin, however, retains: 'Every Scripture is inspired of God, and profitable,' etc. On this it is to be remarked that, whichever form is adopted, the sense is not essentially altered. The form 'Every Scripture inspired of God is also profitable' may be a broader, but it is certain that it is not intended to be a *narrower*, form of statement than the other. The apostle assuredly does not mean to draw a distinction between a Scripture which is inspired, and a Scripture which is not

inspired, or to suggest that any of the 'sacred writings' of the previous verse fall into the latter category.[1] Such an idea is totally foreign to his thought. What he plainly means is that 'every Scripture,' as being inspired (θεόπνευστος), is also profitable.

3. That for which inspired Scripture is 'profitable' is thus described: 'For teaching, for reproof, for correction, for instruction in righteousness; that the man of God may be complete, furnished completely into every good work.'

The doctrine of the passage, then, may be thus briefly summed up:—

(1) There is a collection of 'sacred writings' which Timothy had known from his childhood. These are, it need hardly be said, the Old Testament Scriptures.

(2) The contents of these books were able to make wise unto salvation through faith in Jesus Christ. To Him they pointed; in Him they were fulfilled; in the light of His appearance and salvation they were now read.

(3) The Scriptures included in this collection were 'God-inspired'—more broadly, 'every Scripture,' which *may* include a Gospel like Luke's (cf. 1 Tim. v. 18), or even Paul's own Epistles (cf. 2 Pet. iii. 15).

(4) As having this character, the Scriptures were profitable for teaching, etc., and had as their end 'that the man of God may be complete, furnished completely unto every good work.' There is no want of the spiritual life which they did not meet.

Paul, it will be observed, does not give any descrip-

[1] Cf. Sanday, *Inspiration*, pp. 88, 89.

tion of the *nature* or *degree* of the inspiration he attributes to the Old Testament (or other) Scriptures. He does not, *e.g.*, say that it secured verbal inerrancy in ordinary historical, geographical, chronological, or scientific matters. But (1) it seems at least clearly implied that there was no error which could interfere with or nullify the utility of Scripture for the ends specified; and (2) the qualities which inspiration is said to impart to Scripture, rendering it profitable in so great and rich a degree, make it clear that the inspiration itself was of a high and exceptional kind.

IV. Inspiration and the Record.

(*A*) The Person.

With these general determinations in view, we now proceed to an examination of the *fact* of inspiration as that meets us in the actual phenomena of Scripture. The chief question which invites attention here is the *general relation to inspiration of its record.* The nature of this relation has already been indicated in speaking of the record of revelation as made, either by the original recipients of the revelation, or by those who stood within the circle of revelation, and were possessed in a special degree of its Spirit. The subject must now be more closely investigated.

A first question arises as to the relation of the *inspired person* to the record. Scripture is spoken of as 'God-inspired'; but it is important to notice that inspiration belongs primarily to the *person*, and to the *book* only as it is the product of the inspired person. There is no inspiration inhering literally in the paper, ink, or type, of the sacred volume. The inspiration was in the soul of the writer; the qualities that are communicated to the writing had their seat first in the mind or heart of the man who wrote. It is on the mind, heart, faculties of the *man* that the Spirit works: the work is inspired as coming from his thought and pen, and as having the power of quickening and awakening a like glow of soul in those who read. This is seen very clearly in considering the inspiration of *genius*, as it appears, *e.g.*, in the works of a Shakespeare, a Milton, or a Goethe. The inspiration in these cases is in the souls of the men, and only derivatively in their writings.

V. (*B*) MATERIALS OF THE RECORD.

A more difficult question arises with respect to the relation of inspiration to the *materials* of the record. It is not uncommon to hear inspiration spoken of as if it rendered the subject of it superior to ordinary sources of information, or at least was at hand to supply supernaturally all gaps or deficiencies in that information. The records of the Bible have only to be studied as they lie before us to show that this is an entire mistake. It was said above that it is reasonable to expect that, if God has given a revelation, He will provide for the knowledge of that revelation being preserved, and handed down in its purity. The facts warrant us in saying that this has been actually done. But this, as has likewise been pointed out, and as the most conservative writers will admit, is the work of *providence* rather than of inspiration. Inspiration does not in any case create the fact-materials it works with. It works with the materials it has received. Its presence reveals itself in the use it makes of the materials, and in the insight it shows into their meaning. This will be seen by looking more carefully at the nature of these materials.

1. In *historical* matters it is evident that inspiration is dependent for its knowledge of facts on the ordinary channels of information—on older documents, on oral tradition, on public registers, on genealogical lists, etc. No sober-minded defender of inspiration would now think of denying this proposition. One has only to look into the Biblical books to discover the abundant proof of it. The claim made is that the sources of information are *good*, trustworthy, not that inspiration lifts the writer above the need of dependence on them. In the Old Testament, for instance, reference is constantly made to older or contemporary writings as authorities for the information given as to the acts of the various kings. Thus, for the history of David, reference is made to three works—the Book of Samuel the Seer, the Book of Nathan the Prophet, the Book of Gad the Seer.[1] For numerous reigns extracts are given from 'the Book of the Chronicles of the Kings of Israel'[2] (or 'of the Kings of Judah,' or 'of the Kings of Israel and Judah'). The Books of Ezra and Nehemiah embody genealogies (thus also Chronicles), letters of Persian kings, and other documents.[3] The Gospel of Luke, in

[1] 1 Chron. xxix. 20; cf. on Solomon, 2 Chron. ix. 29; on Rehoboam, 2 Chron. xii. 15, etc.

[2] The quotations from this large work, under one or other of its titles, occur more than thirty times in the Books of Kings (*e.g.*, 1 Kings, xiv. 19, xvi. 20). Also repeatedly in the Books of Chronicles (2 Chron. xx. 34, xxvii. 7, etc.).

[3] Ezra ii. 22, iv. 8-22, viii. 1, etc., Neh. vii. 5, 64, etc.

the New Testament, explains distinctly the manner in which that book was composed, viz., by accurate research into those things which had been delivered to the Church by first-hand witnesses. 'Forasmuch,' says the evangelist, 'as many have taken in hand to draw up a narrative concerning those matters which have been fulfilled among us, even as they delivered them unto us, who from the beginning were eyewitnesses and ministers of the word, it seemed good to me also, having traced the course of all things accurately from the first, to write unto thee in order, most excellent Theophilus, that thou mightest know the certainty concerning the things wherein thou wast instructed.'[1] Where sources of information fail, or where, as may sometimes happen, there are *lacunae*, or blots, or misreadings of names, or errors of transcription, such as are incidental to the transmission of all MSS., it is not to be supposed that supernatural information is granted to supply the lack.[2] Where this is frankly acknowledged, inspiration is cleared from a great many of the difficulties which misapprehension has attached to it.

2. This principle applies not only to historic, but to *prehistoric* times, where written records altogether fail. It does not follow that a sound tradition in essential things may not have been preserved from the beginning. On the Biblical representation of man's origin and relation to God, and of a line of blessing from the earliest age, it may be presumed that it would be. But that tradition will necessarily differ in character from the tradition of historical times, when language, arts, and letters are in some

[1] Luke i. 1-4. [2] See further below, pp. 179-80.

degree developed. It will be couched in part in the forms of thought and speech characteristic of the childhood of the world. As the hieroglyphic precedes alphabetic writing, so the media of transmission of the knowledge of events will be of necessity poetical, symbolical, pictorial, imaginative. This is to be distinguished from 'myth,' which is a pure creation of the imagination, and not the medium of the knowledge of an actual transaction. The example in Scripture is the early chapters of Genesis. The theory at present prevailing, that these chapters —the story of creation and paradise, antediluvian lists, flood, etc.—are based on Babylonian myths, appropriated and purified by the spirit of revelation in Israel, falls below the mark of dignity in the narratives. It is truer to regard them as the embodiments of the earliest and most precious traditions of the race, in the purer form in which they descended through the ancestors of the Hebrew people. They may, however, be ancient, and yet bear traces of transmission in a more or less allegorical or symbolical form. Few, *e.g.*, will be disposed to take literally the account of the making of Eve out of the rib taken from Adam's side while he slept.[1] The story of the Fall, again, may well be the account of an actual historical catastrophe in the commencement of the race, in its cradle in the region of the Tigris and Euphrates.[2] Truths of eternal moment may be enshrined, it is believed are, in its simple narrative. Yet, with many of the most devout expounders of the story, we can hardly err in seeing symbolical elements, or an allegorical dress, in the features of the serpent, the trees, the cherubim.

[1] Gen. ii. 21-5. [2] Gen. ii. 8-15.

The cherubim, throughout Scripture, are *ideal* figures.[1] While, again, remarkable longevity may have been, and probably was, characteristic of the oldest race of men, there is, even in the most conservative circles, a growing consensus of opinion that the early genealogies cannot be interpreted with modern literality—that chronology demands an extensive lengthening of the pre-Abrahamic period, and that the names given in the lists stand rather for representatives of tribes, or clans, or for heads of families, than for individuals.[2] The genealogies also are obviously reduced to a technical scheme in which many links may be omitted. These chapters, nevertheless, embody valuable ancient material, picturing the earliest age of humanity, and conveying profound truths, which inspiration can appropriate, and utilise for its own ends.

The words of Herder on these early chapters of Genesis may here be recalled. 'This is a wonder,' he says, 'to which the worshippers of reason have not yet given a name—the story of the fall of the first man. Is it allegory—history—fable? And yet there it stands, following the account of the Creation, one of the pillars of Hercules, beyond which there is nothing—the point from which all succeeding history starts. . . . And yet, ye dear, most ancient and undying traditions of my race—ye are the very kernel and germ of its most hidden history. Without you, mankind would be, what

[1] On the cherubim, cf., as an older writer, Dr. P. Fairbairn, *Typology of Scripture*, i. pp. 222 ff.

[2] Cf., *e.g.*, Dr. A. A. Hodge, *Outlines of Theology* (1879), p. 297; Dr. W. H. Green, *Bib. Sacra*, April 1890; Dr. J. D. Davis, in his *Dict. of Bible*, art. 'Chronology.'

so many other things are—a book without a title, without the first leaves and introduction. With you our race receives a foundation, a stem and root, even in God and in father Adam.'[1]

This principle applies, finally, to the relations of inspiration to *scientific* knowledge. The Bible is not, nor was ever intended to be, an anticipative text-book of science. This is evident on the face of it. Where natural phenomena are described, it is as they appear to the natural observer. There is no pretence of acquaintance with our modern astronomy, geology, physics, or biology; or with modern scientific classifications of plants and animals. The standpoint is religious—the creation of the world by God, its dependence on Him, His universal activity in it and providence over it. These conceptions stand on a distinct footing from details of science. They have their origin in no source lower than revelation, and carry in them already the outlines of a cosmogony such as we have in the opening chapter of Genesis. If there is so little real conflict—one would rather say so remarkable a harmony—between the Biblical representations and science, it is because the Bible, at the outset, has got the right *standpoint* for the contemplation and interpretation of nature—the true key for the unlocking of its riddle. Without seeking a visional or other special origin for the narrative in Genesis, this at least may be asserted: that the sublimity, freedom from mythology, monotheism, and general agreement with scientific truth of the Genesis account puts it on a totally different plane

[1] *Aelteste Urkunde des Menschengeschlechts* (quoted by Auberlen, *Div. Revelation*, p. 188, which also consult on this subject).

from all heathen cosmogonies. It is related to the Babylonian myth by contrast rather than by resemblance.

VI. (*C*) Literary Form of the Record.

A last question relates to the relation of inspiration to *the literary form* of the record. The chief point to be laid stress on here, in opposition to mechanical views of inspiration—now, however, seldom entertained—is, that inspiration does not annul any power or faculty of the human soul, but raises all powers to their highest activity, and stimulates them to their freest exercise. It is not an influence acting on the soul as a passive instrument, as a player might draw music from a harp, but a life imparted to the soul which quickens it to its finest issues. It follows that there is no form of literature capable of being employed by the genius of man which inspiration cannot employ as its medium. Every one recognises this to some extent in the variety of styles and forms of composition in the Bible. We have in its pages historical narrative and biography; poetry in psalm, hymn, song; gnomic wisdom in proverbs; didactic and doctrinal composition in the epistles; hortatory discourses and appeals; parable and allegory; apocalyptic vision. Each writer in these departments has his own style and idiosyncrasies of thought and treatment. His genius is enkindled, not suppressed, by the power of the Holy Spirit inspiring him.

This principle of the free use by the Spirit of every form of literature will, in the main, be accepted by all; and hesitation need not be felt in carrying out the principle to its fullest extent. Some have scrupled to admit this.

1. There is the form of *drama*. Job, *e.g.*, is a great dramatic poem; one of the grandest in literature. It turns, on the human side, on the possibility of disinterested piety; on the divine side, on the vindication of the divine righteousness and goodness in the permission of the sufferings of the righteous. Its plan is carried through in a prologue, setting forth the theme of the Book; in dialogues between Job and his friends, in the noblest style of poetry; and in an epilogue, restoring the union of virtue and happiness in the return of Job's prosperity. Inspiration could not have found a nobler medium for the inculcation of its lesson; yet some have shrunk from admitting the dramatic form of the work, lest it should detract from the truthfulness of its contents. One has only to ask—How could an accurate report of these long, sustained discourses be obtained or preserved? to see the untenableness of the opposite supposition.

2. There is, again, the form of composition which consists in presenting a theme in *the dress of a speech or treatise* of some person of repute. Few, probably, will dispute that this is a legitimate mode of composition, if used simply as a literary form, without attempt to deceive. As such it is often employed in ordinary literature. No one, *e.g.*, objects to such a work as Landor's *Imaginary Conversations*. Where, on the other hand, there is a deliberate attempt to deceive by passing off one man's work as the production of another, as in Macpherson's *Ossian*, the practice is condemned. It is 'forgery.' The same principle must be applied in judging of Holy

Scripture. If a writing is intended to deceive, there is pseudonymity in the bad sense, and this, one cannot but judge, the Spirit of inspiration must exclude. Simply as a form of literary composition no legitimate exception can be taken to it. Critics as conservative in tendency as Hengstenberg and Keil, *e.g.*, admit this to be the character of the Book of Ecclesiastes. The Book is a didactic work composed in the name of Solomon. Most modern critics regard the Book of Deuteronomy as either a free literary composition of this kind, or at least a free reproduction of speeches traditionally attributed to Moses. Many things, however, have to be taken into account before this can, to the extent claimed, be conceded: the testimony of the Book itself, the archaic character of its contents, the circumstances of its discovery, its unequivocal acceptance as a Book of Moses in the age of Josiah.[1] Many who take this view frankly stamp the Book as a pseudograph. This would, on the principle here stated, be fatal to its inspiration. It is sounder to argue that the manifest inspiration of the Book affords warrant for the rejection of the theory of its fraudulent character.[2]

3. Under this principle of dramatic representation may be brought the *didactic expansions* of speeches, as in the Books of Chronicles—the speech of Abijah,[3] for example—where the homiletic aim of the book has to be considered. In modern preaching on the characters and events of the Bible the same thing is continually witnessed. Scenes are depicted; and the thoughts, feelings, and supposed actions of the

[1] Cf. *Problem of the O.T.*, ch. viii.

[2] The same remark may apply to the Second Epistle of Peter.

[3] 2 Chron. xiii. 1-12.

persons are dramatically exhibited.[1] The genius of the Hebrew language in using direct speech ('He said,' 'Then answered they,' etc.), where a modern would use the indirect form (*oratio obliqua*), not professing to give the exact words, contributed to this form of composition. Especially is this dramatic form of narration inevitable in matters handed down by oral tradition, and acquiring a particular form by repeated telling. There is no more charming idyll than the story of the meeting of Abraham's servant with Rebekah in Gen. xxiv. But certainly there was no stenographer at the well-mouth or in Laban's house to take down *verbatim* reports of the conversations between the parties. This does not militate against the exquisite literary form, or essential truth, of the narrative, but it means that the form in which it reached the narrator was that which it had acquired in long-preserved tradition. Still less can it be claimed that *verbatim* reports are preserved of conversations in Eden, or from days before the Flood. The *substance* belongs to antiquity; the form is that assumed in traditional transmission.

4. Another literary form frequently used in Scripture—pre-eminently in the discourses of Jesus—is *parable*, and, as before seen, commentators are not a little exercised as to whether some of the descriptions in the prophets—*e.g.*, Hos. i.—given in the form of narrative, are not really parabolic or visionary. Many modern interpreters maintain that the Book of Jonah, with its story of 'the great fish,' is really, and in design, a parabolic work. With-

[1] The late D. L. Moody was an expert at this dramatic form of Biblical story-telling.

out questioning that parable is, for prophetic purposes, an admissible form of teaching, one would like to feel surer that the application of the principle in this case is not simply a way of escaping from a felt difficulty in the contents of the Book. The Book of Jonah teaches certainly the loving regard of God for the heathen, but it is in no way clear that the Book is intended as a parable to teach this lesson; still less that the fish incident is an allegory of the swallowing up of Israel by heathenism, etc. Chap. ii. apart, the Book—entirely different in cast from the Jewish 'Haggada'—reads like a piece of serious history, and is, so far as one can see, meant to be so accepted. There is a verisimilitude in the account of Jonah's preaching in Nineveh which forbids its rejection off-hand as fiction. Ch. i. 17; ii. 10 has a different character, and *may* be emblematic of some deliverance, the exact nature of which was not known, but the memory of which is preserved in the verses of the psalm (ii. 1-9). But many will feel that they could accept even the difficulty of the 'fish' more readily than they could reject the historicity of the entire book. Emblem or history, the incident appears in the New Testament as the foreshadowing of a greater event than itself—a 'sign.'[1]

5. A more delicate point arises when it is asked how far *legend* may be employed by inspiration as a vehicle of instruction. Here again there is room for distinction. Legend in itself is a legitimate form of literature, and few preachers or orators would hesitate to introduce a beautiful or appropriate legend to adorn their speech or convey a moral.

[1] Matt. xii. 39-41.

What is open to the preacher now in proclaiming the word of God can hardly be thought of as inadmissible to the divine Spirit in preparing a Scripture for the world. There is, however, a very clear difference between the use of legend for ornament, or for purely literary purposes, and the passing off of legend as a substitute for historic truth. A literary use of legend may be permissible; [1] it may be not unlawful, even, to use narratives into which legendary elements have crept, provided the substance of the narrative is true, and the truth to be conveyed remains unaffected. It is a very different matter when, as in some theories, practically the whole history is converted into legend, and the foundation-facts on which revelation rests are assailed, or converted into fictions, inventions, and imaginations of men. This happens, *e.g.*, when the whole patriarchal history, and the larger part even of the Mosaic history, are converted into legend; or when, in the New Testament, the incidents in the life of Jesus, including His miracles and resurrection, are resolved into myth, or Babylonian fable. Against such tendencies strong protest must be entered. The spirit of the Bible is *truth*, and history is a thing sacred in its eyes. The Bible is jealous of its historical truthfulness, and few books have stood the most rigorous tests applied to their statements, even in regard to the remotest times, better than the Bible has done.

[1] *E.g.*, legendary allusions seem to be found in the Epistle of Jude (vers. 3, 14, are drawn from Apocryphal sources).

CHAPTER IX

INSPIRATION—THE SCRIPTURAL CLAIMS

THE foregoing remarks on inspiration have proceeded on the basis that the inspired record must be, and is, sufficient to convey to us, in purity and faithfulness, the whole will of God for our salvation and guidance. But the course of the discussion, and survey of the Biblical facts, suggest also certain *limitations* with which the doctrine of inspiration, in its application to the several parts of Scripture, must necessarily be received. This is an aspect of the subject which, as arising out of the *data* presented in Scripture itself, likewise requires attention.

I. LIMITS OF BIBLICAL INSPIRATION.

The limitations attaching to inspiration arise from the causes already specified—the *progressiveness* of revelation, the varying *degrees* of inspiration, and the *fragmentariness* or other defects of the materials with which inspiration deals.

1. A first important principle in this connection is, that inspiration *cannot transcend the existing stage of revelation*, in the sense of wholly rising above the imperfections of that stage, even although, in prophetic anticipation, a higher stage may be foreshadowed. This is only to say, in harmony with what was formerly advanced on the progressiveness of revelation, that, while, at every stage, an ennobling and

purifying light is shed by inspiration on the whole field of conceptions then existing, the record is necessarily marked by whatever imperfections still inhere in these conceptions. The Mosaic stage of revelation, *e.g.*, did not clearly condemn polygamy or slavery, though it held in it (already, as Jesus shows of marriage, in the narrative of creation) [1] ideas and principles which effectively wrought for the abolition of both. The Song of Deborah is an inspired production—Deborah is a 'prophetess' [2]—but parts are on the lower key of the rude age of the Judges. There are portions of the Psalms—prayers for the destruction of enemies and imprecatory psalms,[3] which no Christian congregation could now sing, or use in any form without excessive spiritualisation. We find in the New Testament that inspired apostles themselves grew in knowledge with regard to circumcision, and the obligation of the law on the Gentiles,[4] and to the end some had wider and some narrower views.[5] Jesus disclaims the imitation by His disciples of the example of Elijah.[6] What was suitable to the age and circumstances of that prophet (Jesus does not condemn Elijah) might not be suitable to a higher dispensation.[7] All this does not detract from the sufficiency of the Biblical record, taken as a whole; it detracts only from the sufficiency of certain portions of it if taken by themselves. The lower stages have to be read in the light of the higher, with the correction which the higher affords. A Christian may uphold the divine

[1] Matt. ix. 3-9. [2] Judges, iv. 4; v. [3] *E.g.* Ps. cix.
[4] Acts x. 14, 15, 28; xi. 8, 9; xv. 6-29; Gal. ii. 12, 13.
[5] Acts xxi. 18, 25. [6] Luke ix. 34-6.
[7] Cf. on John the Baptist, Matt. xi. 11.

authority of the Old Testament, but he will not feel that he is bound by the Mosaic law of divorce. Jesus did not come to destroy the law or the prophets, but to fulfil them.[1] But the fulfilment was itself an abrogation of whatever was imperfect in the earlier stages.

2. A second important limitation in the application of the idea of inspiration arises from the recognition of *degrees in inspiration*. The doctrine of degrees in inspiration has been wrought out, occasionally with great minuteness, in the older theology; but it is in a somewhat different sense the term is used now. The doctrine need not be viewed with jealousy, or stumbled at, if properly explained and reasonably guarded. It is implied, as already said, in any true doctrine of inspiration, that the record of revelation must emanate from one possessed in a special degree of the Spirit of revelation, qualifying him for his task; but it does not follow that all inspired persons possess the Spirit in a *like* eminent degree. Inspiration in Scripture is of different kinds, and for different ends. It is certainly too narrow an idea of inspiration to tie it down to the production of the written record. There is inspiration in speech as well as in writing; and there are lower grades of inspiration in the form of special *charismata* (wisdom, artistic skill, physical powers), shading off till it becomes difficult to distinguish them from heightened natural endowment. A special inspiration, *e.g.*, is ascribed to Bezaleel for the construction of the tabernacle.[2] Samson's possession by the Spirit took the form of supernatural strength.[3]

[1] Matt. v. 17, 18.
[2] Ex. xxxv. 30, 31.
[3] Judges xiii. 24, 25; xiv. 18; xv. 14, etc.

But, keeping to inspiration in its relation to the written record, can it be doubted that like distinctions are to be recognised? The difference may depend on the subject of inspiration himself or herself;—a Deborah, *e.g.*, stood on an immensely lower plane than an Isaiah or a Paul; or it may depend on the greater or less energy of the working of the Spirit at particular periods or under particular conditions. Laws are at work here, as in the varying degrees in the intensity of the operation of the Spirit in the history of the Church (Revivals), which we can only imperfectly comprehend. But the fact is obvious that, whereas at some periods and in some souls the Spirit of revelation is working, if one may so say, at a maximum, at other times, and in other persons, He is operating on a lower plane, and, still to speak reverently, with feebler energy. Every one, by a species of 'higher criticism' of his own, recognises this in practice, whatever he may do in theory. No one, *e.g.*, would compare the Books of Chronicles, in point of spirituality, with the prophecies of Isaiah or the Gospel of John, or the books of Esther and Ecclesiastes, as to the canonicity of which the later Jews themselves had doubts, with the Epistles of Paul. The prophets after the exile stand, on the whole, on a lower plane than the earlier prophets—Hosea, Amos, Isaiah, etc. In the natural body, as Paul reminds us,[1] all members have not the same office, and so is it here. Some parts of Scripture have a humbler function to fulfil than others. It may be a very real and necessary function, but it is not the highest. The level of truth in one place is not as high as in others.

[1] Rom. xii. 4; 1 Cor. xii. 12-26.

To get the *whole* truth we have to take the record in its entirety, comparing part with part. The Epistle of James may be as necessary a part of a complete Scripture as the Epistles of Paul, but the doctrine of justification would not be understood from the Epistle of James alone.

3. As a third limitation in the application of the idea of inspiration, account has to be taken also of the character and quality of *the sources of information* inspiration has to work with, and of the fact that, while adequate for the ends of revelation, these sources, judged by a literary standard, may be in various ways *defective.* Inspiration, it has been seen, has its materials furnished to it. These materials come in various ways, often through secular channels. There may be gaps or omissions in the information conveyed. In minor respects, as in the copying of MSS., mistakes may have crept into them. The writers of the historical books (Samuel, Kings, Chronicles) used, as we found, earlier documentary material,—prophetic memoirs, state chronicles, histories of kings, lists, genealogies, etc. It is this which gives the books the high historical value they possess. If, however, these prophetic memoirs, lists, etc. were transmitted in MS. form, as they must have been, the MSS. were obviously open to the ordinary mishaps of transmission. Names and numbers might get corrupted, no doubt often did, before the inspired author was reached. It is often said that inspiration only guarantees freedom from all mistake in the original autograph. But in the cases supposed there is a long previous history of documents to be considered. This, in turn, may affect the inspired writer's own

treatment, as, *e.g.*, in the computation of the synchronisms in the Books of Kings, where an error, due to corruption in the regnal years of any of the kings (Pekah's twenty years in 2 Kings xv. 27, *e.g.*, is shown by the Assyrian synchronisms to be a mistake) may throw the reckoning out of step. Genealogical lists, again, may readily be fragmentary, torn, or illegible, in the form in which they came into the hands of the sacred writers, as was manifestly the case in some of the lists in Ezra, Nehemiah, and Chronicles. Is inspiration to take responsibility for these defects? Or is a supernatural communication to be assumed, in each case, to supply the missing word, or correct the misspelt name or corrupted number? This cannot be reasonably maintained, nor does the result in the books show that such correction was made. It did not need to be for the ends of inspiration. Matthew Henry's suggestive remarks on this head have been quoted by the author in another connection.[1] This devout writer, commenting on 1 Chron. viii. 1-32, observes: 'As to the difficulties that occur in this and the foregoing genealogies we need not perplex ourselves. I presume, Ezra took them as he found them in *the books of the Kings of Israel and Judah* (ch. ix. 1), according as they were given in by the several tribes, each observing what method they thought fit. Hence some ascend, others descend; some have *numbers* affixed, others *places*; some have historical remarks intermixed, others have not; some are shorter, others longer; some agree with other records, others differ; some, it seems likely, were torn, erased, and blotted, others more legible.

[1] *Prob. of O. T.*, pp. 486-7.

Those of Dan and Reuben were entirely lost. This holy man wrote as he was moved by the Holy Ghost; but there was no necessity for the making up of the defects, no, nor for the rectifying of the mistakes of these genealogies by inspiration. It was sufficient that he copied them out as they came to hand, or so much of them as was requisite for the present purpose, which was the directing of the returned exiles to settle as nearly as they could with those of their own family, and in the places of their former residence.'

The general phenomena which have to be dealt with in framing a doctrine of the inspiration of Scripture have thus been briefly sketched. More special points will arise as the subject is further treated. It now remains to be asked how far the conclusions reached are in harmony with the teachings and claims of Scripture itself as to its own inspiration, and what kind of doctrine of inspiration answers best to both requirements—the Scriptural claims, and the actual phenomena of the book.

II. Claim to Inspiration. (*A*) The Old Testament in the New.

A first question is—Is any *claim* made in Scripture itself to an inspiration of the book as a whole, and in its several parts? If there is, what is the nature of the claim, and what weight is to be given to it?

In seeking an answer to this question, one fact confronts us at the outset. No claim to inspiration made in the Bible—even in such a passage as 2 Tim. iii. 15-17—can be regarded as covering the whole of Scripture as we have it. This for the simple reason that the Bible as a completed book did not then exist. Plainly 'the Scriptures,' in the usage of the Gospels and the Epistles, can, with the exception of 2 Pet. iii. 16, where Paul's Epistles are included and possibly 1 Tim. v. 18, only be interpreted of the Old Testament. The expression, however, does include the Old Testament writings, according to the ordinary Canon of the Jews, which may be taken as practically identical with our own. It does not follow that these passages have no bearing on the writings of the New Testament, or furnish no guidance as to the estimate to be put on these. Few, probably, will admit a supernatural inspiration for the Old Testament and deny it to the New. An Old Testament Scripture settles the question of *principle* as to an inspired record of revelation. Reasons may be shown for bringing the New Testament writings under the same category; the statements of Jesus and His apostles will then be of validity for the New Testament also.

1. Beginning, then, with the *Old Testament*, it may be regarded as universally conceded that, in the time of Jesus and His apostles, the books we call canonical were accepted by the Jewish people as in the full and true sense '*God-inspired*.' The Sadducees, indeed, accepted only the 'law,' and there were disputes among a section of the Rabbis as to Ecclesiastes and Esther; but no such doubts existed in the minds of the bulk of the people, and certainly none existed in the minds of the writers of the New Testament. Modern writers may question whether the view of Jesus and His apostles was a correct one, but they will not question that the view was there.

2. One crucial passage affirming this belief, 2 Tim.

iii. 15-17, has already been considered. It really embodies the consentient New Testament doctrine on the subject. Everywhere a code of writings is recognised bearing the designations of 'the Scriptures,'[1] the holy Scriptures,'[2] 'the sacred writings,'[3] —the same which the Jews technically divided into 'the law, the prophets, and the (holy) writings,'[4]— and everywhere, in direct speech or by implication, these writings are treated as the 'God-inspired' and authoritative record of God's revelations to, and dealings with, His ancient people. They are, as Paul names them, 'the oracles of God.'[5] It is thus, also unquestionably, that Jesus received the Old Testament. The Synoptics and John are at one in their teaching here. The 'law' was to Jesus 'the commandment of God,' as contradistinguished from the 'tradition' of men,[6] and 'one jot or one tittle,' He declared, would not pass from it 'till all things be accomplished.'[7] Prophecies and psalms were fulfilled in Him.[8] 'The Son of Man goeth,' He declared, 'even as it is written of Him.'[9] His appeal was always to Scripture, and the word of Scripture was final with Him. 'Have ye not read?'[10] 'Ye do err, not knowing the Scriptures, nor the power of God.'[11] This, because 'God' speaks in them.[12] 'Ye search the Scriptures,' He says to the Jews, 'because ye think that in them ye have eternal life; and these

1 Matt. xxi. 42; Luke xxiv. 27.
2 Rom. i. 2.
3 2 Tim. iii. 15.
4 Cf. Luke xxiv. 44.
5 Rom. iii. 2.
6 Matt. xv. 6, 9.
7 Matt. v. 18.
8 Luke xviii. 31; xxii. 37; xxiv. 27, 44.
9 Matt. xxvi. 24; Mark xiv. 21.
10 Matt. xix. 4.
11 Matt. xxii. 29.
12 Ver. 31; cf. Christ's answers to the tempter, Matt. iv. 4, 6, 7.

are they which bear witness of me.'[1] 'If ye believed Moses, ye would believe me; for he wrote of me.'[2] He draws the most pregnant principles and lessons from the sacred history—even from its earliest parts.[3] David spake 'in the Spirit.'[4] 'The Scripture,' He avers, as common ground between Him and the Jews, 'cannot be broken.'[5] The Jews are those 'unto whom the word of God came.'[6] No doctrine of inspiration, surely, could be more emphatic.

3. Yet Jesus, as Founder and Lord of a new dispensation ('the Kingdom of Heaven'), did not accept the Old Testament unconditionally, as if the stage of revelation represented in it were perfect, or was not, with His coming, to give place to a higher. The dispensational imperfections of the Old Testament are fully recognised. He took up, therefore, as Son of Man, a lordly and discretionary attitude towards its letter, laws, and institutions. This is seen in His teaching on such subjects as marriage and divorce,[7] the Sabbath,[8] clean and unclean in meats,[9] etc. He fulfilled, but in fulfilling, necessarily superseded and abolished much in the legal economy. The precepts of the law received a deeper and fuller interpretation and expression, in agreement always, however, with the law's own underlying principles.[10]

4. Taught by Jesus, and possessed of the Spirit promised to them,[11] the apostles and other New

[1] John v. 39.
[2] Vers. 46, 47; cf. Luke xvi. 31.
[3] Matt. xix. 4-6 (marriage); xxii. 31, 32 (resurrection); Matt. xxiv. 37, 38; Luke xvii. 26-32 (Noah, Lot).
[4] Matt. xxii. 43.
[5] John x. 35.
[6] *Ibid.*
[7] Matt. xix. 8, 9.
[8] Mark ii. 27, 28.
[9] Mark vii. 18, 19.
[10] Matt. v. 12; xxii. 35, 40.
[11] Luke xxiv. 49; John xvi. 26; xx. 22; Acts ii.

Testament writers accept and treat the Old Testament precisely as Jesus did. The inspiration of the Old Testament Scriptures is constantly assumed, though, naturally, the apostolic witness relates chiefly to the prophets and psalms.[1] The Messianic interpretation of Scripture employed by them is the continuation of that employed by Jesus Himself. The Spirit of Christ spake in the prophets.[2] The word of Scripture is a word of the Holy Spirit.[3] Scripture, comprehensively, is 'God-inspired.'

III. (*B*) The Old Testament Claim in General.

1. The above testimonies, which could be greatly multiplied, seem sufficiently explicit. The question which will now be asked is, whether they are borne out by *the claims* which the Old Testament *makes for itself*. That the Jews believed in the inspiration of their sacred writings is allowed. Do the New Testament passages prove more than that Jesus and His apostles shared the belief of their nation? It might perhaps be answered that, in the Christian Church, at least, the Old Testament can never mean less to Christ's disciples than it meant to Christ Himself. The question is, however, a fair one as to the compatibility of the claim made for the Old Testament in the passages cited with the witness of the book itself. And here many doubts may be suggested. The Old Testament, like the New, is not a single work, but a collection—a library

[1] Acts i. 16; ii. 16 ff.; iii. 18, 24; Rom. i. 2; iii. 21; xvi. 26; 1 Cor. xv. 3, 4; Heb. iii. 6 ff.; 1 Pet. i. 2; Rev. xix. 10.

[2] 1 Pet. i. 11.

[3] Acts xxviii. 25; Heb. iii. 7; vi. 11. etc.; 2 Pet. i. 20.

—of books. The origin of many of these is obscure; some appear to make no claim to inspiration; most were brought together and acquired canonical authority only at a late period. Where is the evidence that this collection of literature as a whole possesses the quality of inspiration claimed for it?

2. At this point the question of the inspiration of the Old Testament becomes implicated with that of canonicity—a subject on which it is not possible here to enter.[1] This only may be said, that, among the causes determining the reception of a book into the Old Testament Canon, belief in the inspiration of the book may be accounted as the chief. This is the reason which Josephus gives for the rejection of later books, viz., 'the exact succession of prophets having been no longer maintained.'[2] The books which *were* received were, according to him, 'justly accredited as divine.'[3] On any other principle it would be difficult to account for the exclusion of such a work as that of the Son of Sirach (Ecclesiasticus), written about 200 B.C., or of compositions like the Psalms of Solomon. While, moreover, many questions regarding the origin of particular books must remain unsolved, the greater part of the Old Testament can be shown by its internal character, by the claims made for it, and by its place in the history of revelation, to be entitled to rank as a work of inspiration.

3. It is a fact of much significance that, in many passages of the Old Testament, we find references to what appears to be a code of sacred writings in use

[1] Cf. *Prob. of O. T.*, pp. 481 ff.
[2] *Contra Apion.*, i. 8. [3] *Ibid.*

among the pious in Israel, through the study of which their minds were nourished, and by meditation on which they were comforted and sustained. Such are the references to the 'law' and 'word' of God, in many of the Psalms. Whatever the date of compositions like Pss. i., xix., cxix., they do not, at least, come down so far as the final closing of the Canon; and no one who reads attentively their eulogies on God's law, and exhortations to meditation on it, and notes the qualities ascribed to the law (enlightening, quickening, converting, cleansing, directing, etc.), can fail to perceive that a very considerable range of literature, in a known form, must already have existed for the godly. It is arbitrary to bring the whole of the Psalms down below the Exile. Ps. i. would seem to have existed before Jeremiah, who quotes it.[1] Ps. xix. has a good claim to be Davidic.

It is not the Psalms themselves, however, that are alone in question; it is the 'law' of God which they presuppose and praise. The attributes ascribed to the law—attributes which only inspiration could impart—can hardly be satisfied by the sacrificial and priestly directions of the Levitical code. Something of wider scope and more spiritual character must be understood. Or take such passages as Ps. xii. 6: 'The words of the Lord are pure words, as silver tried in a furnace, purified seven times'; or Ps. xvii. 4: 'By the word of Thy lips, I have kept me from the ways of the violent'; or the references to God's 'ways,' 'ordinances,' 'statutes,' in Ps. xviii. 21, 22 (by the highest title Davidic), and the inference must be the same. The

[1] Jer. xvii. 8.

psalmists had sure 'words' of God,—tried words, rules and laws for life, on which they could rely with certainty as coming from Jehovah.

Other parts of the Old Testament present similar indications. Job is exhorted to 'receive the law from [God's] mouth and lay up His words' in his heart;[1] and the patriarch replies: 'His way have I kept, and turned not aside. I have not gone back from the commandment of His lips: I have treasured up the words of His mouth more than any necessary food.'[2] In Proverbs we read: 'Every word of God is tried. . . . Add thou not to His words, lest He reprove thee, and thou be found a liar.'[3] Where were these life-giving words to be found, if not in some form of Scripture? So Isaiah can appeal 'to the law and to the testimony,'[4] and can exhort his readers: 'Seek ye out of the book of the Lord, and read: no one of these shall be missing, none shall want her mate.'[5] Jeremiah can speak of a 'law of the Lord,' which false pens had falsified.[6] Hosea, speaking for Jehovah, mourns: 'I wrote for him the ten thousand things of my law; but they are counted as a strange thing.'[7] Daniel consults 'the books' for the number of the years set for the desolation of Jerusalem,[8] and speaks of that which was 'written in the law of Moses, the servant of God.'[9] In brief, Scriptures, which must have contained the records of God's dealings with His people, a knowledge of which is constantly presupposed, 'laws' of God for the regulation of the heart and conduct, 'statutes,' 'ordinances,'

[1] Job xxii. 22. [2] Job xxiii. 11, 12. [3] Prov. xxx. 5, 6.
[4] Is. viii. 20. [5] Is. viii. 20. [6] Jer. viii. 8.
[7] Hos. viii. 12. [8] Dan. ix. 2. [9] Vers. 11-13.

'words' of God, are a postulate of a great part of the Old Testament.

IV. (*C*) Old Testament Claim—The Several Parts.

It is necessary now to approach nearer, and ask whether any of these inspired Scriptures can be more closely identified. And here another fact which meets us is, that, if the testimony of the Old Testament itself be taken—and it is that we are now dealing with, not theories about the Old Testament—a large part of the materials of the Old Testament *do* come from men who were indubitably, and in the highest sense, inspired.

1. This appears in part from the character of the material; but it appears also from what is expressly stated. *The law*, as a whole, claims divine authority. As a whole, also, it claims to emanate from Moses. Grant, if it is thought necessary, that it may have undergone revision, codification, editing, at later times, by competent authority—for only under such authority could changes gain acceptance—it is still 'the book of the law of Moses' as far back as we can trace it.[1] Parts of it are attested in a special manner. The Book of the Covenant, *e.g.*, is expressly said to have been written by Moses at the forming of the covenant with Jehovah at Sinai.[2] The Book of Deuteronomy is likewise said — the discourses contained in it at least are—to have been written by Moses, and formally delivered by him to the priests.[3] Whether the book in its existing form is

[1] Josh. i. 7, 8; viii. 30, 35; xxiv 26· 2 Kings xiv. 6; Neh. viii. 1; Dan. ix. 11-13, etc.

[2] Ex. xxiv. 4, 7.

[3] Deut. xxxi. 9, 24.

this very work, or a more or less expanded reproduction of it by a later prophet, is a secondary question; the inspiration of the book is felt in every verse and line. Joshua, similarly, is declared to have written in 'the book of the law of the Lord.'[1]

2. Taking next the extensive *prophetic* literature of the Old Testament, it will not be denied that *this* claims to be produced under direct divine inspiration. The prophets are *the* inspired men, *par excellence*, of the Old Testament. Called and equipped for their special work by God, endowed with a special measure of His Spirit, receiving their messages from His hand, delivering them under the solemn sanction of a 'Thus saith the Lord,' accrediting them with supernatural prediction, they speak and write with an authority which cannot be taken from them. Their writings, accordingly, answer in the highest degree to the tests of inspiration.

3. The prophets, however, were more than preachers; they were the *historians* in Israel. History, in the Old Testament, in its conception, genesis, spirit, execution, is of necessity *sacred* history. It is never a mere record of secular events, but is a history of revelation,—such, therefore, as only men of a prophetic spirit could produce. The Jews indicated their sense of this fact, and the idea under which the historical books were accepted into the Canon, by designating the series from Joshua to 2 Kings (Ruth excepted) 'the former prophets.' The prophets, in fact, seem all along to have acted as the sacred 'historiographers' of the nation, writing monographs on particular reigns, or histories of events contemporary, or nearly so, with themselves.

[1] Josh. xxiv. 26.

This is fully borne out by the notices in the later books, already alluded to, of the prophetic sources from which the longer narratives are compiled.[1] While the prophetic compositions were themselves in circulation, they would, in their separate form, to some extent serve the purpose of Scripture. It was needful, however, that in the end longer histories should be drawn up; and, though we cannot now trace the steps by which these sacred documents were collected, the essential parts extracted from them, and the whole brought together in the setting which exhibited the divine meaning, we may see in the product that this task also was carried through by prophetically minded men, themselves deeply imbued with the spirit of the history they recorded. It is this prophetic character of the books which gives them their claim to a place in an inspired collection.

The same remark applies to the earlier history in the Pentateuch. The Book of Genesis is a history of revelation till the death of Joseph. The remaining books record, along with the legislation, the events of the Mosaic period—that formative period in Israel's history. These books form really part of the 'law,' the foundations of which, if not much more, Moses, the most gifted of prophetic spirits, is credited with laying. If Joshua, on whom the spirit of Moses rested,[2] and others like-minded, collaborated or continued the work, the reality of its inspiration, internally attested by its massive unity, insight, and pervasion by the great ideas of revelation, is not affected.

[1] See above, p. 164. Cf. Kirkpatrick, *Divine Library of O. T.*, pp. 13 ff.; Ottley, *Aspects of O. T.*, p. 145 ff., etc. [2] Josh. i. 1-9.

4. The Psalms, which exhibit rather than declare their inspiration, have already been spoken of; but one passage, which may be regarded as typical of their standpoint on this subject, represents David as saying, 'David the son of Jesse saith. . . the Spirit of the Lord spake by me, and His word was upon my tongue.'[1] The Wisdom-literature has its classical form in the Book of Proverbs, and is there put forth, not as a product of man's genius, but as an utterance of the Eternal Wisdom, the outpouring of whose Spirit is promised.[2]

V. New Testament Inspiration.

1. If a seemingly disproportionate attention has been bestowed upon the Old Testament, it is for the reason already given, that few who acknowledge a divine inspiration in the Old Testament will be disposed to deny it to the New. The apostles are placed by Jesus Himself in the category of prophets,[3] again are raised above the prophets of the Old Testament.[4] It is promised that, in their need, the Spirit of the Father will speak in them.[5] Especially in the farewell discourses of Jesus is the Spirit promised to guide them into all truth, and to bring all things to their remembrance, whatsoever He had said to them.[6] The outpouring of the Spirit on the disciples—

[1] 2 Sam. xxiii. 2. Dr. Sanday remarks: 'We have to note that there are a number of instances in which the Psalmist adopts forms of language which we are accustomed to associate specially with prophecy,' and refers for instances to Dr. Cheyne's *Aids to Devout Study*, etc., p. 152 (*Inspiration*, p. 195).

[2] Prov. i. 20 ff.; viii. 1; 'prophecy,' xxx. 1. Cf. 1 Kings iii. 5-15.

[3] Matt. xxiv. 34. [4] Matt. xi. 11; xii. 17, 52. [5] Matt. x. 20.

[6] John xiv. 26; xv. 26, 27; xvi. 13, 14.

pre-eminently on the apostles—at Pentecost, with its remarkable results in illumination of the mind and endowment with spiritual and miraculous power, shows in how signal a way this promise was fulfilled.[1] The Spirit was the element in which the early Church lived. Baptism of the Spirit, with accompanying gifts, frequently followed baptism and the laying on of hands.[2] The apostles, and men like Stephen, are spoken of as 'filled with the Holy Spirit,'[3] and as discoursing under His influence. Revelations, prophecies, tongues, were no uncommon phenomena.[4] It is understood, rather than always claimed, that writings emanating from apostles and those associated with them possessed the quality of inspiration.

2. The writings of the New Testament have only to be examined to make clear, not only the light and power which are the supreme attestation of their inspiration, but the pervading assumption, and often open assertion, of their unique and authoritative character as inspired writings.[5] Paul's apostleship was based upon a special call and a distinct mission, for the carrying out of which he had special promises and special qualifications given to him ('filled with the Holy Spirit').[6] He never faltered in his claim to be 'an apostle of Jesus Christ, by the will of God'[7]—'separated unto the Gospel of God'[8]—who had received his message, not from man, but by 'revelation' from heaven.[9] In his preaching he

[1] Acts ii. etc.
[2] Acts viii. 15-17, etc.
[3] Acts ii. 4; iv. 8; vii. 55, etc.
[4] 1 Cor. xii.
[5] 1 Cor. ii. 4-10; 1 Thess. i. 5; ii. 13; 1 John iv. 6; Rev. xxii. 19, etc.
[6] Acts ix. 17.
[7] Eph. i. 1, etc.
[8] Rom. i. 1.
[9] Gal. i. 11, 12.

claimed to possess the Spirit,[1] and to speak 'the word of God,' in the fullest and most authoritative sense.[2] John makes similar claims to the possession of the Spirit, enabling him to understand and to write the truth so that no one is at liberty to gainsay.[3] He claims, indeed, for his hearers a like 'unction,' qualifying them to understand and judge of the truth,[4] as Paul prays that a 'spirit of wisdom and revelation' may be given to his converts.[5] But the apostles are the *teachers*; their converts and disciples are the *taught*. Peter writes with a like clear note of certainty, as of one who preached the Gospel 'by the Holy Spirit sent down from heaven.'[6] The Apocalypse is a product of the Spirit of prophecy—a 'revelation.'[7] In general—and stronger language could not be used—the 'mystery of Christ' has 'now been revealed unto His holy apostles and prophets in the Spirit.'[8] In consequence, the Church is declared to be 'built upon the foundation of the apostles and prophets, Christ Jesus Himself being the chief corner stone.'[9]

3. These illustrations suffice to show in how special a manner inspiration is claimed for the apostolic writings, and in how real a sense these are entitled to be brought under the category of 'Scripture'—as, indeed, Paul's Epistles already are in 2 Pet. iii. 16. The character of New Testament inspiration will receive further elucidation in the next chapter, but a word may perhaps be said here

[1] 1 Cor. ii. 12, 13, 16.

[2] Rom. x. 8; 2 Cor. 1, 18; v. 19; 1 Thess. ii. 13; iii. 14; Col. i. 25, etc.

[3] 1 John iv. 6; v. 15, 19, 20.

[4] 1 John ii. 20, 26-7; iv. 6.

[5] Eph. i. 17.

[6] 1 Pet. i. 12.

[7] Rev. xxii. 19; cf. i. 1-3.

[8] Eph. iii. 5.

[9] Eph. ii. 20.

on the inspiration of those who stand in a *secondary* relation to the apostles—writers, *e.g.*, like Mark and Luke. On what grounds, or in what sense, is inspiration to be attributed to them? The inspiration of the Gospels by these writers, as will be seen later, does not rest solely on the inspiration of their immediate authors. Much of their content is the well-attested and internally confirmed teaching of Jesus Himself: their substance, almost entirely, is that compendium of sayings and events, resting on testimony of apostles and eye-witnesses, which had taken well-fixed shape as the result of Spirit-guided apostolic teaching and preaching long before the evangelists brought it into its present written form. But the evangelists were none the less themselves inspired men. They were men who belonged to the apostolic circle, and stood in a peculiar relation of intimacy with the apostles, sharing in their work, and, as the whole conditions of the Church in that age prove, possessing in a special degree gifts of the Spirit.

This is an interesting point. A comparison of the facts relating to the companions of the apostles—to Silas, Timothy, Mark, Luke, in particular—did space permit of it, would show how broad a basis for the claim to inspiration could here be laid. One need only recall the manner in which Paul habitually associates such men with himself in the most sacred and responsible functions of his ministry,—how he writes, *e.g.*, 'For the Son of God, Jesus Christ, who was preached among you by me, even by me, and Silvanus and Timothy, was not yea and nay,' [1]—how he joins the same two with him in his epistolary

[1] 2 Cor. i. 19.

greeting to the Thessalonians, and says: '*Our* Gospel came not unto you in word only, but also in power, and in the Holy Spirit,' [1]—how he repeatedly dwells on 'the gift' which Timothy had received, with prophesyings, by the laying on of hands,[2]—to see that Mark and Luke must have been sharers of a like consecration and like gifts,[3] qualifying them for the special work they were ultimately to undertake. The Spirit's guidance, which was not wanting in every step of an apostle's journey,[4] was not likely to be lacking when the life of the Master came to be written. And the result shows beyond controversy that it was not.

[1] 1 Thess. i. 1, 5.
[2] 1 Tim. i. 18; iv. 14; 2 Tim. i. 6, 14.
[3] Cf. Acts xii. 25; xiii. 1, 2, 5; xv. 36-41, etc.
[4] Acts xvi. 7, etc.

CHAPTER X

INSPIRATION—RESULTS FOR DOCTRINE OF HOLY SCRIPTURE

It is now time to gather up results, and ask whether a doctrine of inspiration is attainable which shall at once be true to the facts of the record and true to the claims of Scripture itself on this important subject. In the answer to this question is involved the answer to another—Is there for the Church of to-day a tenable doctrine of Holy Scripture ?

I. Revelation and Inspiration—Their Relations.

1. It will have been seen that it is sought in the preceding pages to approach the subject of inspiration through that of *revelation*. This seems the right method to pursue. The doctrine of inspiration grows out of that of revelation, and can only be made intelligible through the latter. The older method was to prove first the inspiration (by historical evidence, miracles, claims of writers), then through that establish the revelation. This view still finds an echo in the note sometimes heard —' If the inspiration of the Bible (commonly some *theory* of inspiration) be given up, what have we left to hold by ? ' It is urged, *e.g.*, that unless we can demonstrate what is called the ' inerrancy ' of the Biblical record, down even to its minutest details,

the whole edifice of belief in revealed religion falls to the ground. This, on the face of it, is a most suicidal position for any defender of revelation to take up. It is certainly a much easier matter to prove the reality of a divine revelation in the history of Israel, or in Christ, than it is to prove the inerrant inspiration of every part of the record through which that revelation has come to us. Grant the Gospels to be only ordinary historical documents—trustworthy records of the life of Christ, apart from any special inspiration in their authors—we should still, one may contend, be shut up as much as ever to the belief that the Person whose words and works they narrate was One who made superhuman claims, and whose character, words, and deeds attested the truth of these claims.[1] It is assuredly easier to believe that Jesus spoke and acted in the way the Gospels declare Him to have done, than to prove that Mark and Luke possessed an exceptional inspiration in the composition of their writings—though, as has been already stated, there is the best reason for believing that they did.

[1] This has often been put as strongly as it can be by the stoutest defenders of the infallibility of Scripture. Cf., *e.g.*, Bannerman, *Inspiration: the Infallible Truth and Divine Authority of the Holy Scriptures*, pp. 18 ff. Drs. Hodge and Warfield, arguing for an 'errorless Scripture,' write: 'Nor should we ever allow it to be believed that the truth of Christianity depends upon any doctrine of inspiration whatever. Revelation came in large part before the record of it, and the Christian Church before the New Testament Scriptures. Inspiration can have no meaning if Christianity is not true, but Christianity would be true and divine, and being so, would stand, even if God had not been pleased to give us, in addition to his revelation of saving truth, an infallible record of that revelation absolutely errorless by means of inspiration' (*Presby. Rev.*, April 1881, p. 227).

2. The same remark applies to the tendency to make 'inerrancy'—*i.e.*, hard and fast literality in minute matters of historical, geographical, and scientific detail—a point in the *essence* of the doctrine of inspiration. The subject will come up later, but at present it may be observed that, at best, such 'inerrancy' can never be demonstrated with a cogency which entitles it to rank as the foundation of a belief in inspiration. It must remain to those who hold it a doctrine of faith; a deduction from what they deem to be implied in an inspiration established independently of it; not a ground of belief in the inspiration.[1] It is, as before, easier to establish the fact of the reality and all-pervading presence of an inspiration adequate to the ends of revelation than to demonstrate this particular aspect of it.

3. But now another fact has to be taken into account. If, on the one hand, it has been seen that, in the order of inquiry, revelation precedes inspiration, it has become not less clearly evident that over a large area, in the fact itself, revelation and inspiration are *closely and inseparably united.* Internal revelation, *e.g.*, such as we have in prophecy, or in the 'revelation of Jesus Christ' claimed for himself by Paul, is not conceivable save as accompanied by an inspired state of soul. Inspiration is involved in the very reception of such a revelation; is a necessary

[1] Bannerman says: 'The unintentional errors which may be and are found in writings marked by perfect historical veracity, cannot be taken account of as affecting the force or conclusiveness of this argument. Making any allowance that can reasonably be demanded for the possibility of such errors, and subtracting from the sacred text what might by any chance be set to that account, there remains enough for the purpose which the friends of inspiration have in view,' etc. (*op. cit.*, p. 284).

condition of the revelation being apprehended, possessed, and communicated to others. In the very acknowledgment, therefore, of revelation as an element pervading the Bible and giving unity to its parts, there is implied an acknowledgment of inspiration. Just as, on the other side, there can be no degree of inspiration, however humble, which does not imply some measure of revelation.

4. Revelation and inspiration thus go together, and conjointly give to the written word *a quality* which distinguishes it from any product of ordinary human wisdom. Inspiration, Paul says, confers on Scripture the properties of being 'profitable for teaching, for reproof, for correction, for instruction which is in righteousness'—of being able 'to make wise unto salvation through faith which is in Christ Jesus.'[1] Of similar nature are the qualities ascribed in the psalms to the law of God—'restoring the soul,' 'making wise the simple,' 'rejoicing the heart,' 'enlightening the eyes,'[2] etc. As Jesus says of His own words, that they 'are spirit and are life,'[3] so of the word of God in general it is declared that it 'is living and active, and sharper than any two-edged sword, and piercing even to the dividing of soul and spirit, of both joint and marrow, and quick to discern the thoughts and intents of the heart.'[4] The last passage is the more significant that, in the context, the writer has been identifying words from the Book of Genesis and the Psalms with words of God and of the Holy Spirit.[5] Paul and John likewise declare that to the spiritual man (and

[1] 2 Tim. iii. 15-17.
[2] Pss. xix. 7-9; cxix., etc.
[3] John vi. 63.
[4] Heb. iv. 12.
[5] Heb. iii. 7-iv. 11.

only to him) belongs the discernment of the word of God.[1]

II. Witness of the Spirit to Inspiration.

1. On this undeniable, self-attesting spiritual quality of Scripture some would lay the whole weight of the proof of inspiration. It is the *testimonium Spiritus Sancti*—the witness of the Holy Spirit—on which Calvin, some of the Reformed Confessions, and a writer like John Owen, would rest almost exclusively the certainty of the divine origin and authority of Scripture.[2] The aim is to obtain a ground for assured faith in God's Word independently of Church and tradition. The Westminster Confession—somewhat broader in its outlook—states the matter in this way: 'We may be moved and induced by the testimony of the Church to an high and reverent esteem of the Holy Scripture, and the heavenliness of the matter, the efficacy of the doctrine, the majesty of the style, the consent of all the parts, the scope of the whole (which is to give all glory to God), the full discovery it makes of the only way of man's salvation, the many other incomparable excellences and the entire perfection thereof, are arguments whereby it doth abundantly evidence itself to be the word of God; yet, notwithstanding, our full persuasion and assurance of the infallible truth, and divine authority thereof, is from the inward work of the Holy Spirit, bearing witness by and with the word in our hearts.'[3]

[1] 1 Cor. ii. 14, 16; 1 John iv. 1-3.

[2] Calvin, *Instit.* I. 7. 4, 5; Helvet. and French Confessions; Owen, *Div. Orig. of Script.*, chs. ii. iv.

[3] Ch. i. 5.

2. The principle here enunciated has undoubtedly wide scope, and may be applied with effect to sustain belief in the inspiration of *parts of Scripture* which do not of themselves directly make such claim—the Psalms, *e.g.*, or certain Epistles, or the Gospels. The New Testament Epistles have only to be compared with the productions of the post-apostolic age,[1] or the canonical with the apocryphal Gospels, to see how immense—in the case of the Gospels how incredibly great—is the descent. It is not simply that the Gospels, as embodying the words of Jesus, and narrating His acts, have a divineness that goes beyond any dignity that inspiration could impart; but the record itself, in its simplicity, manifest fidelity, self-effacement of the human author, pervasive sense of the divine greatness of One, to the significance for the world of whose appearance the wise men of the age were so utterly blind, compels the acknowledgment that more than human care and skill were involved in its production—that the finger of God is there! If the other internal evidences are added,[2] a strong argument may be built up, not only for the reality of revelation in Scripture, but for an inspiration in the books in which that revelation is conveyed.

3. It must still be confessed that the principle here employed may be *pushed too far*, and made to sustain conclusions which cannot in justice be

[1] The Early Fathers, as will be seen, were fully conscious of this difference.

[2] In his (posthumous) work on *Inspiration*, Dr. F. Watson, of Cambridge, justly lays stress on the evidence from the Biblical Doctrine of Sin (ch. vii.), the Harmony of the Teaching (viii.), the Purity of the Teaching (ix.), the Abidingness of the Teaching (x.), etc.

rested on it. How, *e.g.*, can it legitimately be employed, taken by itself, to sustain the canonicity, not to say the inspiration, of books like the Song of Solomon, Esther, or Ecclesiastes, which belong, in the opinion of some, to the lowest grade of inspiration; or, still further, to establish a perfectly 'errorless' record?[1] The principle, in fact, may be, and often has been, applied in a quite opposite direction, viz., to warrant the rejection of all parts of Scripture which do not appeal to the individual mind, or, as Coleridge says, 'find' it. One recalls here Luther's rejection of the Epistle of James as 'an epistle of straw,' because he did not find in it Paul's doctrine of justification. Richard Baxter, one of the saintliest of men, thus wrote: 'I confess, for my part, I could never boast of any such testimony or light of the Spirit or reason; neither of which, without human testimony or tradition, would have made me believe that the book of Canticles is canonical and written by Solomon, and the book of Wisdom apocryphal and written by Philo, as some think, or that Paul's Epistle to the Laodiceans and others is apocryphal, and the second and third Epistle of John canonical. Nor could I ever have known all or any historical books, such as Joshua, Judges, Ruth, Samuel, Kings, Chronicles, Ezra, Nehemiah, to be written by divine inspiration, but by tradition,' etc.[2] This may be

[1] Cf. Bannerman, *op. cit.*, pp. 270-1, who points out this weakness. In the view of the present writer, the Book of Esther, which Dr. Sanday puts lowest, gets scant justice from some of its critics. It is a wonderful record of God's providence. The permission given to the Jews to defend themselves (Esth. viii. 11; ix. 1, 2) is not to be confounded with the decree to massacre issued earlier at the instance of Haman (iii. 13). Cf. Dr. Sanday's note, *op. cit.*, pp. 222-3.

[2] Preface to Second Part of *Saints' Rest.*

felt to carry objection too far on the other side; but the fact that a man like the author of *The Saints' Everlasting Rest* could write in this strain shows the precariousness of the principle as one on which to rest the whole Biblical case for inspiration. Many evidences converge to sustain inspiration—internal witness, testimony of the books, use by other Scriptures, witness of Christ and His apostles, effects and fruits in experience and history—and all are to be welcomed.

4. The inspiration which gives its distinctive quality to Scripture, as claimed for its writings by Jesus, by prophets and apostles, and often by the books themselves, is not of a kind that can properly be paralleled by human *genius*, or even by the ordinary illumination of Christians. It is sometimes said: 'Isaiah was inspired as Shakespeare, Burns, Scott, or Carlyle was; Paul was inspired as Luther or Mazzini was.' But could any of these gifted men have prefaced their utterances, as the prophets did, with a 'Thus saith the Lord'; could it be said of the greatest of them what is said of New Testament apostles and prophets, that a Church was founded on their witness? 'Built upon the foundations of the apostles and prophets. . . . The mystery of Christ, which in other generations was not made known unto the sons of men, as it hath now been revealed unto His holy apostles and prophets in the Spirit.'[1] The Spirit is given to all Christians, but in diversity of measures, and with specific gifts. And what ordinary Christian will feel that he could use language about himself like the above!

[1] Eph. ii. 20; iii. 4, 5. Cf. Dr. Sanday on 'Modern Prophets, *op. cit.*, pp. 166-7.

III. Inspiration in History.

1. For further light on the nature of inspiration one turns naturally to *history*, to inquire what views on the subject have been entertained, inside the Church and out of it, at different periods. Ideas of both revelation and inspiration, as before seen, are not wanting in heathenism. Analogies drawn from these foreign sources, however, are apt to mislead oftener than to help. No heathen religion possesses that which is the fundamental presupposition of Biblical inspiration—a living God, and a community within which the Holy Spirit of God is continuously active. The sporadic oracles of heathenism—pythonic responses and the like—assuming these to be as genuine as they were generally spurious, had nothing in common with this continuous, growing form of revelation through chosen, inspired organs. Neither is the analogy required furnished by the 'sacred books' of other religions. The 'Rishis' of the Vedas do not claim for themselves more than a poetical inspiration. Buddha's 'enlightenment' was no inspiration from above, for his system had in it no place for either God or Holy Spirit. The Gathas or hymns which form the oldest parts of the Zend-Avesta are put into the mouth of Zoroaster. They contain invocations and prayers for enlightenment, and Ahura answers; but this is probably not more than literary form. The Confucian classics make no claim to inspiration. Mohammed, of course, claims that the messages combined in the Koran were communicated to him by direct revelation, and his claim must be

treated on its merits; but few, treating it impartially, will be disposed to concede it. The Bible makes no claim for the origin of its books such as is made for the Koran—that their parts came down in external revelation from heaven,—and the claim if made, could not be entertained.

2. Philo and Josephus sufficiently attest the belief in the inspiration of the Scriptures among the Jews. The early Rabbis held the same doctrine.[1] Josephus connects inspiration with the prophetic gift; Philo, the earlier of the two, borrows from heathen mantic the idea of ecstasy, in which the individuality of the inspired man is wholly suppressed, and his soul reduced to pure passivity. This, it has been seen, is far from the conception of inspiration in the Bible itself. It is a position now universally recognised by writers on the subject that inspiration does not suppress individual genius, but heightens and develops it. All the powers that lie in a man's natural endowment, the gains of his training, the results of his experience, are laid hold of, and fused into a new unity round the central point of the new revelation that is given to him. Self-consciousness, the power of self-control, are not lost. 'The spirits of the prophets are subject to the prophets.'[2] This, too, in the main, is the doctrine of the early Church. That the early Fathers, in the most emphatic way, maintained the complete inspiration of the Holy Scriptures, Old

[1] See in detail on the teaching of Philo and Josephus in the works on Inspiration by Sanday, Lee, Bannerman, Watson, etc. On the Rabbinical views, cf. Sanday, pp. 80-2, 90: 'What might be thought somewhat strange, the disputed books [Eccles., Song, Esther] seem to be used quite as freely as the rest.'

[2] 1 Cor. xiv. 32.

Testament and New, no one acquainted with their writings will deny;[1] and if the favourite illustration of the lyre and plectrum may appear to lean to a view akin to Philo's of the suppression of the human consciousness, the general trend of their teaching will show that this is by no means the intention.[2] Montanism, which took this view, was rejected. Origen, in particular, contends strongly against the comparison of Jewish prophecy to the frenzied utterances of the Pythian prophetess.[3] He holds for himself the strictest doctrine of inspiration, getting over the contradictions and other difficulties which he allows to exist (really, and not merely, as some say, 'apparently') in the historical and prophetic parts by the aid of his allegorical method of interpretation.[4]

The opinions of the Reformers on inspiration have frequently been discussed. There is a singular breadth and modernness in Calvin's exegesis; but his faith in the entire inspiration of the Scriptures is profound and uncompromising. The ultimate guarantee of inspiration, as already seen, is found by him in the internal witness of the Holy Spirit.[5] The creeds of the Reformed Church embodied the same conceptions. Occasionally divines carried

[1] The testimony of the Early Church is very fully exhibited in Westcott's *Introd. to the Study of the Gospels*, Appendix B. A long catena of passages is given in Lee, Appendix G. Clement of Rome says: 'The blessed Paul at the beginning of the Gospel in very truth wrote by inspiration' to the Corinthians. Ignatius says: 'I do not give you injunctions as Peter and Paul; they were apostles, I a condemned man.'

[2] Athenagoras is an exception. He speaks of the prophets as 'entranced and deprived of their natural powers of reason.'

[3] *Contra Celsum*, vii. 4.

[4] *De Princip.* iv. 1; *Contra Cels.* iv. 48.

[5] *Instit.* I. 7. 4, 5.

them to extremes that never obtained general sanction.[1] Luther's views, as his ordinary teaching and use of Scripture show, were scarcely less high; but, applying a subjective standard, his judgments on certain books, as the Epistle of James, Revelation, Esther, even the Epistle to the Hebrews, were rash and arbitrary.[2] These judgments affected canonicity rather than inspiration. Sometimes Luther is misjudged, as, *e.g.*, when Dr. F. Watson states: 'He described the argument St. Paul derived from Hagar and Sarah in the Galatians as too weak to hold.'[3] This is a mistaken statement, as any one will see who reads what Luther really wrote on what he calls 'this goodly allegory,' 'a wonderful allegory,' praising the apostle for his use of it. What he does say is: 'For if Paul had not proved the righteousness of faith against the righteousness of works by strong and pithy arguments, he should have little prevailed by this allegory. But, because he had fortified his cause before with invincible arguments . . . now, in the end of his disputations, he addeth an allegory, to give beauty to all the rest. For it is a seemly thing sometimes to add an allegory,' etc.[4] There is no suggestion of any feebleness in Paul's inspiration.

Later views came gradually to prevail, especially through Arminian influence, and modern opinions

[1] *E.g.* The younger Buxtorf (followed by the 'Formula Consensus Helvetica') affirmed the inspiration of the Hebrew vowel points.

[2] 'He was as thoroughly convinced of the inspiration and authority of the Word of God as the most orthodox divine can be, but he had free views on the mode of inspiration and the extent of the traditional canon' (Schaff, *Creeds of Christendom*, i. 215).

[3] *Inspiration*, pp. 232-3.

[4] *Com. on Gal.* iv. 24, etc.

have already been adverted to. Disputes turn largely in recent times on what is named 'verbal' inspiration, and on the degree to which 'inerrancy,' or complete freedom from error or contradiction in matters not directly involved in the substance of the inspired teaching, is implied in inspiration.

IV. 'Verbal Inspiration.'

1. The phrase 'verbal inspiration' is one to which so great ambiguity attaches that it is now very commonly avoided by careful writers.[1] There is, indeed, a sense in which the phrase expresses a true and important idea. It opposes the theory that revelation and inspiration have regard only to thoughts and ideas, while the language in which these ideas are clothed is left to the unaided faculties of the sacred penman. This is a defective view. Thought of necessity takes shape and is expressed in words. If there is inspiration at all, it must penetrate words as well as thought, must mould the expression, and make the language employed the living medium of the idea to be conveyed.[2] The Scripture lays stress upon the *words*—often on the

[1] *E.g.*, by Lee, Bannerman, etc. The former prefers 'plenary,' the latter 'dynamical.' Hodge and Warfield defend the word 'verbal,' but with careful explanation. 'There is the more excuse,' they say, 'for this misapprehension because of the extremely mechanical conceptions of inspiration maintained by many former advocates of this term "verbal." This view, however, we repudiate as earnestly as any of those who object to the language in question' (*op. cit.* p. 233).

[2] 'The slightest consideration,' says Dr. Westcott, 'will show that words are as essential to intellectual processes as they are to mutual intercourse. . . . Thoughts are wedded to words as necessarily as soul is to body' (*Study of Gospels*, p. 14).

very form of the expression. 'We speak,' says Paul, 'not in words which man's wisdom teacheth, but which the Holy Spirit teacheth.'[1]

2. 'Verbal inspiration,' however, is often taken to mean much more than this. It is apt to suggest a *mechanical* theory of inspiration, akin to dictation, which all intelligent upholders of inspiration now agree in repudiating. In the result it may be held to imply a *literality* in narratives, quotations, or reports of discourses, which the facts, as we know them, do not warrant.

(1) A very evident illustration of the untenableness of this theory is in the *reports of the Lord's own sayings* in the Gospels. It is well known that in the reports of Christ's words in the Synoptic Gospels there is often a very considerable variation in expression—a difference in phraseology—while yet the *idea* conveyed in all the forms is the same. At most one side or another of the truth is brought out with slightly different emphasis. In illustration, let the version of the Lord's sayings in the Sermon on the Mount in Matthew be compared with that in Luke,[2] and the wide divergence in expression, with identity in idea, will at once be seen. Here the advocates of verbal inspiration are themselves compelled to recognise that absolute literality is not of the essence of inspiration—that the end is gained if the *meaning* of the saying is preserved, though the precise form of words varies. There may be compression, combination, change of construction—even (as in John) interpretation; but the truth is purely given.

(2) Another palpable illustration of this freedom

[1] 1 Cor. ii. 13. [2] Matt. v.-vii.; Luke vi. 20-40.

in regard to the letter, while the sense is accurately conveyed, is found in the New Testament *quotations* from the Old Testament. In these, it is again well known, great variety in the method of quotation prevails. Sometimes, where the end is better served, the quotation is taken directly from the Hebrew (*e.g.*, Matt. ii. 15) ; occasionally the translation is free (Matt. ii. 6) ; ordinarily the quotation is made with more or less exactness from the Greek version—this even where the Hebrew is somewhat widely departed from (Matt. xii. 17-21 ; Rom. ix. 33 ; 1 Pet. ii. 6 ; Heb. x. 5-7, etc.). Inspiration here again must be held compatible with a want of literality in the words.[1]

3. In view of these facts, it is felt by many that, to express the idea of an inspiration which pervades all the parts of the record, the word '*plenary*' is more suitable than 'verbal.' This term, while doing justice to the freedom of the sacred writer in his use of language, argument, and illustration, in the employment of his faculties in research, and in his methods of using his material, avoids the mistake into which others fall of speaking as if *parts* of the record were inspired, and *parts* uninspired. The passages usually quoted in support of this view are Paul's words in 1 Cor. vii. 10, 12, 25 : 'Unto the married I give charge, yet not I, but the Lord. . . . But to the rest say I, not the Lord. . . . Concerning virgins I have no commandment of the Lord, but I give my judgment.' These verses, however, are not valid to establish any such distinction as is alleged. What Paul means to say is only that he had no direct 'command' from the Lord for what he said—no

[1] See further on this point, *The Bible under Trial*, pp. 268 ff.

word of Jesus spoken while on earth—such as he had in the case of marriage. Yet Paul claimed that he had 'the Spirit of God' in giving his judgment on the cases before him;[1] nay, goes so far as to declare: 'If any man thinketh himself to be a prophet, or spiritual, let him acknowledge of the things which I write unto you, that they are the commandments of the Lord.'[2]

V. 'Inerrancy' of the Record.

While, by most of the older writers, the inspiration of the entire record in the Bible is strenuously affirmed, great diversity of view prevails as to the *mode* of the action of the divine influence by which this result is secured. Theories of dictation of historical matter, or of communication of facts that could be ascertained by ordinary methods, are now universally surrendered;[3] the distinction of 'revelation' and 'inspiration' is better recognised; but whereas some would lay chief stress on the exaltation of the human faculties, and conscious direction and 'suggestion,' others are content to resolve inspiration into a divine 'superintendence,' often unconscious, leaving everything else—and this the greater part—

[1] Ver. 40. [2] 1 Cor. xiv. 37.

[3] The slight qualifications of this which Dr. Lee (p. 147) and others make, *e.g.*, in the supernatural communication to Paul of the institution of the Lord's Supper (Bannerman, p. 189), rest on a misunderstanding. Paul undoubtedly 'received' the Lord's words at the Supper from the apostles or general tradition.

Hodge and Warfield lay stress on this human side. 'Each drew from the stores of his own original information, from the contributions of other men, and from all other natural sources. Each sought knowledge, like all other authors, from the use of his own natural faculties of thought and feeling,' etc. (p. 229).

in the production of an 'errorless' record to 'providence.'[1] The question which here arises is—Does the Bible itself claim, or inspiration necessitate, such an 'errorless' record, in matters of minor detail? The discussion may close with a few words on this subject of 'inerrancy.'

1. Very commonly it is argued by upholders of this doctrine that 'inerrancy' in every minute particular is involved *in the very idea* of a book given by inspiration of God. This might be held to be true on a theory of verbal dictation, but it can scarcely be maintained on a just view of the actual historical genesis of the Bible. One may plead, indeed, for 'a supernatural providential guidance' which has for its aim to exclude all, even the least, error or discrepancy in statement, even such as may inhere in the sources from which the information is obtained, or may arise from corruption of anterior

[1] This is the thesis, elaborated with much fulness, of Hodge and Warfield. 'We intentionally,' they say, 'avoid applying to this inspiration the predicate "influence." It summoned, on occasion, a great variety of influences, but its essence was superintendence. This superintendence attended the entire process of the genesis of Scripture, and particularly the final composition of the record. . . . The Scriptures were generated through sixteen centuries of this divinely regulated concurrence of God and man, of the natural and supernatural, of reason and revelation, of providence and grace. . . . The natural knowledge came from all sources, as traditions, documents, testimonies, personal observations, and recollections, . . . yet all were alike under the general direction of God's providence. The supernatural knowledge became confluent with the natural in a manner which violated no law of reason or of freedom. And throughout the whole of His work the Holy Spirit was present, causing His energies to flow into the spontaneous exercises of the writer's faculties, elevating and directing where need be, and everywhere securing the errorless expression in language of the thought designed by God. This last element we call inspiration' (pp. 226, 229, 231).

documents. But this is a violent assumption which there is nothing in the Bible really to support. It is perilous, therefore, to seek to pin down faith to it as a matter of vital moment. Inspiration, in sanctioning the incorporation of an old genealogy, or of an historic document in some respects defective, no more makes itself responsible for these defects than it does for the speeches of Job's friends in the Book of Job, or for the sentiments of many parts of the Book of Ecclesiastes, or for the imperfect translation of Old Testament passages in quotations from the Septuagint.

2. Even on the assumption of a 'verbal' inspiration, it has been seen in how wide a sense *literal accuracy* in the Biblical records has to be interpreted. The theory may be stretched, moreover, by qualifications, admissions, and explanations, till there is *practically* little difference between the opposite views. Thus, writing on the New Testament quotations, with reference to the objection of Dr. S. Davidson that, on the theory of verbal inspiration, the New Testament writers should have adhered to the *ipsissima verba* of the Holy Spirit in the Old Testament, seeing these were best, the able defenders of an 'errorless' record already repeatedly cited remark: 'Here, however, a false view of inspiration is presupposed, and also a false view of the nature and laws of quotation. Inspiration does not suppose that the words and phrases written under its influence are the best possible to express the truth, but only that they are an adequate expression of the truth. Other words and phrases might be equally adequate:—might furnish a clearer, more exact, and therefore better

expression, especially of those truths which were subordinate or incidental for the original purpose of the writings.'[1] It would be difficult, however, to show that this superiority always belongs to the LXX. renderings adopted. More generally, we have such wide acknowledgments as the following: 'It is not claimed that the Scriptures any more than their authors are omniscient. The information they convey is in the forms of human thought, and limited on all sides. They were not designed to teach philosophy, science, or human history as such. They were not designed to furnish an infallible system of speculative theology. They are written in human languages, whose words, inflections, constructions, and idioms bear everywhere indelible traces of human error. The record itself furnishes evidence that the writers were in large measure dependent for their knowledge upon sources and methods in themselves fallible, and that their personal knowledge and judgments were in many matters hesitating and defective, or even wrong.' So much being admitted, it hardly seems worth while to deny the compatibility of inspiration with the possibility of minor errors also in the *matter* of the record. Yet 'the *ipsissima verba* of the original autographs' are held to be free from the slightest taint of such error.

3. These things have in justice to be said on the one side. On the other side, one finds himself in substantial harmony with the defenders of this view in affirming that *the sweeping assertions* of error and discrepancy in the Bible often made cannot be substantiated. Ascribe it to 'providence,'

[1] Hodge and Warfield, *op. cit.* p. 256.

to 'superintendence,' to 'suggestion,' or what one will,—and inspiration is probably more subtle and all-pervading than any of these things,—it remains the fact that the Bible, impartially interpreted and judged, is free from demonstrable error in its statements, and harmonious in its teachings, to a degree that of itself creates an irresistible impression of a supernatural factor in its origin. It is of little profit to discuss such a subject as 'inerrancy' in the abstract. When the objector descends from generalities to details, one knows where to find him; and here, in cases without number, it has been shown by the progress of knowledge that it is *he*, not the Bible, that is wrong. Many of the alleged discrepancies are such only in appearance, or are readily explained by difference in point of view or aim, or from technicalities of structure, as in genealogies, or from methods of grouping and generalising, where precise detail is not aimed at. Some are due to corruption in the texts—this frequently in names and numbers—either in the existing texts, or possibly in the MSS. sources used by the sacred writer himself. Archæology has brought confirmation to the statements of the Bible, even in its oldest parts, in a multitude of particulars in which its accuracy had been confidently challenged. Illustration of these assertions has been furnished in abundance elsewhere.[1] When, in smaller matters, discrepancy is urged, as, *e.g.*, in the various reports of the titles of the Cross, it is time for the discussion to stop.

4. On this broad, general ground the advocates

[1] See, in illustration, *Prob. of O. T.*, ch. xi.; *The Bible under Trial*, chs. vi., xi.

of 'inerrancy' may always feel that they have *a strong position*, whatever assaults may be made on them in matters of lesser detail. They stand undeniably, in their main contention, in the line of apostolic belief, and of the general faith of the Church,[1] regarding Holy Scripture. The most searching inquiry still leaves them with a Scripture, supernaturally inspired to be an infallible guide in the great matters for which it was given—the knowledge of the will of God for their salvation in Christ Jesus, instruction in the way of holiness, and the 'hope of eternal life, which God, who cannot lie, promised before times eternal.'[2]

VI. Conclusion.

This leads, in closing, to the remark that, in the last resort, the proof of the inspiration of the Bible —not, indeed, in every particular, but in its essential message—is to be found in the life-giving effects which that message has produced, wherever its word of truth has gone.[3] This is the truth in the argument for inspiration based on the witness of the Holy Spirit. The Bible has the qualities claimed for it as an inspired book. These qualities, on the other hand, nothing but inspiration could impart. It leads to God and to Christ; it gives light on the deepest problems of life, death, and eternity; it discovers the way of deliverance from sin; it makes men new creatures; it furnishes the

[1] This is shown, as respects the Early Church, in the copious extracts compiled by Dr. Westcott and by Archdeacon Lee in their appendices to their works formerly referred to (p. 207).

[2] Titus, i. 2.

[3] Col. i. 5, 6.

man of God completely for every good work.[1] That it possesses these qualities history and experience through all the centuries have attested; its saving, sanctifying, and civilising effects among all races of men in the world attest it still. The word of God is a 'pure word.'[2] It is a true and 'tried' word;[3] a word never found wanting by those who rest themselves upon it. The Bible that embodies this word will retain its distinction as *the Book of Inspiration* till the end of time!

[1] 2 Tim. iii. 17.
[2] Pss. xii. 6; xix. 8; cxix. 140, etc.
[3] Ps. xii. 6; xviii. 30.

BIBLIOGRAPHY

The following books may be referred to :—

Rothe, *Zur Dogmatik*, (Pt. II., 'Revelation'; Pt. III., 'Holy Scripture'), 2nd Edit., 1869.

Ewald, *Revelation: Its Nature and Record*, E. T., 1884.

Dorner, *A System of Christian Doctrine*, E. T., vol ii., Div. III. ('The Doctrine of Religion,' 'The Doctrine of Revelation, 1881).'

Oehler, *Theology of the Old Testament*, E. T., vol. i. (Pt. I., 'Of Revelation'), 1874.

Auberlen, *The Divine Revelation*, E. T., 1874.

Orelli, *Old Testament Prophecy* ('Introduction'), 1893.

A. B. Davidson, *Old Testament Prophecy*, 1903.

G. T. Ladd, *The Doctrine of Sacred Scripture*, vol. i., 1883.

A. B. Bruce, *The Chief End of Revelation*, 1881.

W. Lee, *The Inspiration of Holy Scripture: Its Nature and Proof*, 1874.

J. Bannerman, *Inspiration: the Infallible Truth and Divine Authority of the Holy Scriptures*, 1865.

A. A. Hodge, and B. B. Warfield, Art. 'Inspiration' in *The Presbyterian Review*, April 1881.

B. F. Westcott, *An Introduction to the Study of the Gospels*, 1872.

R. F. Horton, *Inspiration and the Bible: An Inquiry*, 1888 ; *Revelation and the Bible: an Attempt at Reconstruction*, 1892 ; *Verbum Dei*, 1893.

W. Sanday, *Inspiration* (Bampton Lectures), 1893.

J. M. Gibson, *The Inspiration and Authority of Holy Scripture*, 1908.

D. M. M'Intyre, *The Spirit in the Word*, 1908.

INDEX